THE END OF ROE

The End of Roe assesses abortion and the American legal and political system in the aftermath of the United States Supreme Court's June 2022 decision in *Dobbs v. Jackson Women's Health Organization.*

In *Dobbs*, the US Supreme Court held that a woman did not have a constitutional right to terminate her pregnancy. This decision further polarized an already divided nation by overturning nearly fifty years of precedent under *Roe v. Wade*, following on from two highly contentious presidential elections. Now, as Christian conservative legal organizations seek to tighten access to abortion through attempts to limit chemical abortion, the most widely used method to terminate pregnancies in the United States, as well as cut off other avenues to the procedure, access to abortion seems uncertain and increasingly complicated across the United States. This book discusses how widely differing abortion laws have evolved across the United States, as well as how religious groups and conservatives have turned to the legal process in their fight to restrict abortion further and how more progressive states have countered with the passage and implementation of safe harbor laws shielding physicians who perform abortions and the women who wish to procure them, mainly when their home state is hostile to their medical situation or choice. This book demonstrates how abortion will continue to shape future elections and the consequences of these political contests on this issue.

This book will appeal to students and scholars of American politics, ethics, politics and religion, and women and politics, as well as practitioners in the areas of law, political science, sociology, and philosophy, and anyone interested in the abortion debate in the United States.

Jeanine E. Kraybill, PhD, JD is a Professor of Political Science and Pre-Law Program Director at California State University, Bakersfield, USA.

Routledge Studies in Religion and Politics

Edited by Jeffrey Haynes,
London Metropolitan University, UK

This series aims to publish high-quality works on the topic of the resurgence of political forms of religion in both national and international contexts. This trend has been especially noticeable in the post-cold war era (i.e., since the late 1980s). It has affected all the 'world religions' (including Buddhism, Christianity, Hinduism, Islam, and Judaism) in various parts of the world (such as the Americas, Europe, the Middle East and North Africa, South and Southeast Asia, and sub-Saharan Africa).

The series welcomes books that use a variety of approaches to the subject, drawing on scholarship from political science, international relations, security studies, and contemporary history.

Books in the series explore these religions, regions, and topics both within and beyond the conventional domain of 'church–state' relations to include the impact of religion on politics, conflict and development, including the late Samuel Huntington's controversial – yet influential – thesis about 'clashing civilisations'.

In sum, the overall purpose of this book series is to provide a comprehensive survey of what is currently happening in relation to the interaction of religion and politics, both domestically and internationally, in relation to a variety of issues.

The End of Roe
The Religious Right's Regulatory Fight Over Reproductive Rights
Jeanine E. Kraybill, PhD, JD

For more information about this series, please visit: https://www.routledge.com/Routledge-Studies-in-Religion-and-Politics/book-series/RSRP

THE END OF ROE

The Religious Right's Regulatory Fight Over Reproductive Rights

Jeanine E. Kraybill, PhD, JD

Routledge
Taylor & Francis Group
LONDON AND NEW YORK

Designed cover image: Getty Images

First published 2026
by Routledge
4 Park Square, Milton Park, Abingdon, Oxon OX14 4RN

and by Routledge
605 Third Avenue, New York, NY 10158

Routledge is an imprint of the Taylor & Francis Group, an informa business

British Library Cataloguing-in-Publication Data
A catalogue record for this book is available from the British Library

Library of Congress Cataloging-in-Publication Data
Names: Kraybill, Jeanine E., author.
Title: The end of Roe : the religious right's regulatory fight over reproductive rights / Jeanine E. Kraybill, PhD.
Description: Abingdon, Oxon [UK] ; New York, NY : Routledge, 2025. | Series: Routledge studies in religion and politics series | Includes bibliographical references and index.
Identifiers: LCCN 2025020522 (print) | LCCN 2025020523 (ebook) | ISBN 9781032636153 (hardback) | ISBN 9781032624693 (paperback) | ISBN 9781032636177 (ebook)
Subjects: LCSH: Abortion—Law and legislation—United States—History. | Reproductive rights—United States—History. | Religious right—United States—History. | Pro-life movement—United States—History. | United States. Supreme Court—Cases—History. | Dobbs, Thomas E.—Trials, litigation, etc. | Roe, Jane, 1947–2017—Trials, litigation, etc.
Classification: LCC KF3771 .K73 2025 (print) | LCC KF3771 (ebook) | DDC 342.7308/4—dc23/eng/20250522
LC record available at https://lccn.loc.gov/2025020522
LC ebook record available at https://lccn.loc.gov/2025020523

ISBN: 9781032636153 (hbk)
ISBN: 9781032624693 (pbk)
ISBN: 9781032636177 (ebk)

DOI: 10.4324/9781032636177

Typeset in Times New Roman
by codeMantra

CONTENTS

Acknowledgment *vii*

1 *Dobbs:* How Did We Get Here? 1

2 Pro-Life Religious Interest Groups and the Regulatory Authority over Reproductive Rights 25

3 *Red States v. Blue States* and the Regulation of Reproductive Rights in a Post-*Dobbs* America 50

4 Access to Chemical and Emergency Abortion Services Post-*Dobbs* 80

5 Dobbs and the Ballot 97

Index *119*

ACKNOWLEDGMENT

I would like to thank my husband, Jesse Kraybill, for his love, support, and continued faith in me.

I would also like to express my gratitude for choice and opportunity, my hope is that all people may experience these blessings, so they can rise to their fullest potential.

1

DOBBS

How Did We Get Here?

On May 2, 2022, "the worst breach of confidentiality in the court's history" became public as *Politico* reported Associate Justice Samuel Alito's leaked opinion on *Dobbs v. Jackson Women's Health Organization* (de Vogue et al., 2023). The leak ignited abortion-rights protests across the country, causing the Supreme Court to take extra security measures (Howe, 2023). For seven weeks, the American people anxiously waited for the Court to release the final opinion, as speculation circulated on whether the decision would overturn nearly fifty years of precedent. On June 24, 2022, the wait was over, and the Court released a repudiating blow to *Roe v. Wade* (1973) and *Planned Parenthood v. Casey* (1992), stating both decisions were overturned because the Constitution did not confer a right to abortion.

With over 60% of Americans stating abortion should be legal in all or most cases at the time of the *Dobbs* decision, how did the Court get here (Pew Research Center, 2022)? Didn't Associate Justice Brett Kavanaugh, who voted with the majority in *Dobbs*, tell the American people during his 2018 Senate confirmation hearing for the Supreme Court that *Casey* was "precedent on precedent" (Liptak, 2018)? To begin to answer these questions, several issues must be examined. First being how abortion politics falls along religious and political lines, especially among evangelical Protestant and conservative Catholic religious elites. Second, how stances on abortion have become sorted between Republicans and Democrats, along with the religious influence that has infiltrated the political party system on this debate. Third, how critical parts of the *Dobbs* decision disregarded the

DOI: 10.4324/9781032636177-1

doctrine of substantive due process, unraveling federal protection to abortion access, setting the stage for more high-stakes reproductive rights battles.

Abortion and Party Politics

The political debate on abortion in the United States has been largely influenced by religious conservatives, particularly within the Catholic Church and among Evangelical Protestants (Scanlon, 2023). To understand this influence, it is important to look at a brief history of both groups' involvement in abortion politics.

Starting in the twentieth century, Evangelical Protestants began to take issue with the teaching of evolution in public schools. A particular instance, the Scopes "Monkey" Trial in 1925, was a catalyst for the beginnings of the Christian Right, a social movement led by religious conservatives that still exists today (Wilcox, 1988; Claassen, 2018; Conger, 2018). The Scopes trial dealt with a substitute teacher, John T. Scopes, who was prosecuted for violating the state of Tennessee's Butler Act, which prohibited the teaching of evolution in public schools. Though Scopes lost at trial, his conviction was overturned by the Tennessee State Supreme Court (Foster, 2009). However, evangelicals still carried influence on the topic, with evolution being effectively banned from biology textbooks across the country for several decades (Claassen, 2018). However, as support for the anti-evolution campaign in public schools subsided, conservative Protestant leaders shifted their attention to an anticommunism theme to combat the belief in atheism, which many communist leaders professed. During this time, Protestant leaders also threw their support behind prohibition and again anticommunism in the McCarthy era (Wilcox, 1998).

However, the Christian Right's fight for influence over education was not done with the Scope's trial. In the aftermath of *Brown v. Board* (1954), the famous Supreme Court ruling desegregating public schools, white evangelicals in the South began creating racially segregated private schools, such as the Lynchburg Christian Academy in Virginia, established Rev. Jerry Falwell in 1967. In response to these private segregation initiatives, Black parents filed lawsuits to enjoin private schools to stop the practice or lose their tax-exemption status with the Internal Revenue Service (IRS). However, the question remained whether religious discrimination was permissible in private school admissions practices. The Supreme Court did not take up the issue until it heard *Bob Jones University v. the United States* (1983), finding the IRS was correct to revoke the school's tax-exempt status for such discriminatory practices (Claassen, 2018). Some argue that it was this case and Ronald Reagan's commitment to protect religious institution's tax-exemption status that helped crystallize the Christian Right's alignment with political conservatives (Claassen, 2018).

However, both conservative Protestants and Catholics were disturbed by the Supreme Court's decision in *Engel v. Vitale* (1962) and *Abington v. Schempp* (1963), which prohibited school-sponsored prayer and reading of the bible in public schools. Furthermore, *Roe v. Wade* (1973), which held that the 9th and 14th Amendment granted a woman a constitutional right to an abortion, up until the point of viability, not only further strengthened the social conservative connection between Evangelical Protestants and Catholics but also began to develop their strong pro-life connection (Payne, 2023).

Though some point to *Roe* as the beginning of Christian conservatives taking on abortion with a pro-life agenda, it is important to recognize the Catholic Church has a long-standing position that life begins at conception and is against abortion (Catechism of the Catholic Church, 2016). The Catholic Church in the United States began speaking out politically on the issue in the 1940s, when the American bishops created a model list of human rights, which included the right to life (Scanlon, 2023). Regarding conservative Protestants, many of the organizations that are affiliated with the Christian Right post-date *Roe*, such as Focus on the Family, founded in 1977, and the Moral Majority, established in 1979 (Claassen, 2018). The Moral Majority arguably became one of the most prominent organizations of the Christian Right, which served as an umbrella association for conservative Protestants, Catholics, and Jews to mobilize voters to elect politicians that would defend their values, especially opposition to abortion and other perceived threats to the family (Payne, 2023).

In looking at how the abortion debate became sorted between the two major political parties, it is also important to note that in the summer before *Roe*, *Gallup* polling reported that 64% of Americans (the majority Catholic) agreed that the decision to have an abortion was solely between a woman and her physician, with more Republicans

(68%) holding this view than Democrats (Greenhouse and Siegal, 2011). So, what are other factors that led anti-abortion positions to become a mainstay for Republican Party politics? Some argue it was a party realignment election strategy by Republicans in 1972, designed to take away Catholic voters from the Democratic Party. For example, in the years leading up to *Roe* (1964 to 1973), more than a dozen states modified restrictive abortion policies. For example, in 1967, Colorado was the first state to decriminalize abortion, permitting it in cases of rape, incest, or a pregnancy that would cause severe physical disability to the woman. In 1970, New York was the first state to legalize abortion through the twenty-fourth week of pregnancy (Baker et al., 2022). Knowing the Catholic Church's pro-life position, Republicans looked to take away Catholic support from social conservatives who were for President Richard Nixon's opponent, George McGovern, in the 1972 election. This realignment began in 1971, with Nixon's shift of position on abortion when he directed the Department of Defense to cancel therapeutic abortions in military hospitals, a position his administration implemented the year prior. Influenced by advisor, Patrick Buchanan, who pressed Nixon that abortion was a growing issue among Catholics, the President became more verbal with his change of position during the election, stating that unregulated and on demand abortion policies were incompatible with the sanctity of human life (Greenhouse and Siegal, 2011; Adams, 1997). To court social conservatives away from the Democratic Party, Republican strategists were able to tie the abortion issue to larger cultural conversations about permissive youth, the erosion of traditional family values, and the loss of respect for authority. Nixon won reelection with most of the Catholic vote, though abortion was not a main determinant for voters. However, the realignment of the Republican Party on the abortion issue was taking shape, especially as support for the Equal Rights Amendment (ERA) was percolating, a constitutional proposal guaranteeing equal legal rights for all citizens regardless of sex (Nixon Library, 2022). In the early 1970s, Republicans such as Richard Nixon supported the ERA, which was even endorsed in the Grand Ole Party (GOP) platform; however, in years shortly after *Roe*, Republicans began to debate more vigorously about family values, the role of women in society, and abortion. Abortion would first be mentioned in the Republican Party platform in 1976, noting the divide between those in support of the procedure and those looking to protect the lives of the unborn (Fisher, 2012).

However, by the late 1970s, not only did Republicans begin to solidify their position on social conservative issues and consolidate electoral support, but they also fostered party discipline in Congress. As noted above, this coincided with Rev. Jerry Falwell and the Moral Majority's desire to maintain their IRS tax-exempt status while resisting racial integration of Christian private schools. Yet, conservatives such as Bob Jones and Jerry Falwell knew that a "Stop the tax on segregation!" was not a winning rallying cry for the broad conservative movement they were working to build in the United States. The more agreeable strategy to build a new Christian Right movement was to consolidate Christian conservative support around abortion, which at first would be challenging given that when *Roe* was decided not only did most Republicans support it, but the Southern Baptist Convention passed resolutions in 1971 and 1974, supporting less restrictive abortion laws, and in 1967, then Republican Governor of California, Ronald Reagan, passed one of the country's most liberal abortion laws (Steward, 2022). As part of a strategy to build a broader Christian Right and evangelical movement in the United States, the Republicans began to embrace the pro-life agenda more fully to promote traditional societal and family values and use it as a tool to divide the base of support in the Democratic Party (Greenhouse and Siegal, 2011; Adams, 1997). During the late 1960s and 1970s, Political Action Committees began to form, such as The National Right to Life Committee (the oldest pro-life lobby in the United States) and The National Association for the Repeal of Abortion Laws (NARAL). With these organizations' fundraising and lobbying ability, congressional votes on abortion became more clearly sorted along party lines with Republicans voting increasingly more pro-life and Democrat pro-choice (Greenhouse and Siegal, 2011; National Right to Life, 2023; NARAL, 2023). And by 1980, the abortion issue was settled among Republicans with their party platform seeking a constitutional amendment to protect the life of the unborn (Fisher, 2012). The abortion debate was now firmly divided between the two major political parties. And the Christian Right was well aware that its best bet to restrict abortion access, and possibly even overturn Roe, was by constructing a strong sphere of legal influence through the development of Christian Conservative Legal Organizations (CCLOs), which would eventually lead to their role in *Dobbs* and a new era of abortion politics.

Christian Conservative Legal Organizations

Scholars, such as Jack Balkin (2024), argue that the *Dobbs* decision was a long-sought goal of the Christian conservative legal movement, following the *Roe* decision and subsequent election of Ronald Reagan. Balkin argues that *Roe* was finally overturned because in 2018, members of the Christian Legal Movement finally dominated the court, and that previously, though Republican Presidents had made more appointments to the Supreme Court from 1969 to 2020 compared to Democrats that not all conservative appointees were affiliated with the movement. Essentially having the additions of Gorsuch, Kavanuagh, and Barett to conservatives, such as Thomas, Alito, and Roberts (though he argues the latter is somewhat institutionally restrained due to his position as Chief Justice), helped *Roe* to get overturned more quickly once three newer associate justices joined this conservative contingent of the Court. Furthermore, Balkin argues that though the majority of American public opinion supports some sort of abortion to be constitutionally permissible, the Supreme Court has become a place of entrenched partisanship where the conservative elites on the bench do not reflect the center of America. He argues that this partisan entrenchment is a result of several key factors. First, Republicans benefiting from Senate malapportionment, which allows states that are less populated to vote more conservatively, hence influencing the makeup of the chamber and influencing federal judicial appointments. Second, Senate Republicans getting rid of the filibuster with Neil Gorsuch's appointment and therefore lowering the super majority threshold vote needed to push nominations to the Supreme Court through. Third, Senate Republicans going back on their word not to consider Supreme Court judicial appointments during election years when Ruth Bader Gainsbourg passed away and Amy Coney Barrett was approved on October 26, 2020, just a week before the 2020 Presidential Election. Balkin argues these events have all been part of the Christian Conservative Legal Movement's vision for a constitutional revolution that brings together the group's concerns over increased secularism, women's liberation, and traditional family values, all under a single issue, abortion, paving the way to overturn *Roe*.

However, the rise of the Christian Legal Movement and the efforts of Christian conservatives to insert themselves more profoundly into abortion and *Dobbs* era politics would not have occurred without the involvement of the Federalist Society. The Federalist Society, formed in 1982 by students at Yale Law School, Harvard Law School, and the University of Chicago Law School, came together with the goal of creating a network among young legal conservatives. The Federalist Society soon morphed into an influential organization that today consists of 90,000 members made up of lawyers, law students, and legal scholars from around the country with student divisions at all 204 American Bar Association–accredited law schools across the country (Balkin, 2024; The Federalist Society, 2024). The Federalist Society touts a commitment to limited government and conservative constitutional principles. The organization does not take official stances on issues of law or policy because its mission is to cultivate and facilitate a conservative legal network that gives its member attorneys access to state legislature and influence in the federal judicial appointment process. Though the Federalist Society claims, "we do not lobby for legislation…or endorse nominees and candidates for public service" (The Federalist Society, 2024), members and leadership actions seem to speak otherwise. For example, Kristen Waggoner, Federalist Society member and general counsel for the Alliance Defending Freedom, worked alongside the state of Mississippi's legal team in preparing for arguments in *Dobbs v. Jackson Women's Health Organization* (Green, 2022). And, Leonard Leo, Co-Chairman and former Executive Vice President of the Federalist Society, drafted lists of potential justices for 2016 Trump Campaign to consider and advised President Trump on the nominations of Neil Gorsuch, Brett Kavanaugh, and Amy Coney Barrett to the Supreme Court of the United States (Kroll et al., 2023). Trump's lasting legacy to the federal judiciary has been largely influenced by the decades of work by the Christian conservative legal movement. From Ronald Reagan to Joe Biden, Donald Trump is the President with the highest number of appointments to the federal bench, at a total of 218 (Heritage Foundation, 2024). With the *Dobbs* decision, this movement achieved its long-term goal of overturning *Roe*. However, the movement has also been focused on other religious liberty rights as well as now restricting access to abortion even more so via challenging the Food and Drug Administration's authorization of the mifepristone, which is discussed later on in this book in detail as well as the outcome of the movements legal case against the government agency.

As discussed above, conservatives were aware that utilizing organizations, such as the Moral Majority, was an important tool for mobilizing Evangelical Protestants and other conservative Christians into politics during the 1980s (Ruby, 2007). However, religious conservatives were also aware that to push their public policy agenda, centered on traditional marriage, religious liberty, and right to life, they would also need to employ a legal strategy where they could influence legislation and take up legal battles in the courts to challenge statues that worked against these initiatives (Cole Smith, 2023; Bennett, 2015, 2017). As Lewis (2017) argues, within the last several decades, conservatives have taken a page out of liberals' playbook in pushing a rights based legal approach. Conservatives have been doing this by turning religion into an individual rights argument in the form of conscientious protection legislation and the enactment of religious freedom restoration acts in conservative states. This has led some conservatives to use legal challenges to push for individual rights for those who personally object to practices, such as abortion. Overall, religious conservatives have seen the need to embark on a more organized and coordinated legal strategy in the aftermath of *Roe*, hence the Christian Legal Movement was born with the development of CCLOs (Bennett, 2015, 2017). The first CCLO, the Center for Law and Religious Freedom, was formed ten years after *Roe v. Wade* (National Catholic Report, 2017). Today, there are several dozen high-profile legal Christian advocacy organizations across the country (Cole Smith, 2023). Many of these CCLOs began with the support of Christian elites who saw the potential positive impact legal advocacy would have for their causes. For example, Pat Robertson established the National Legal Foundation and the American Center for Law and Justice, while James Dobson, Dennis James Kennedy, and Bill Right were pivotal in organizing the Alliance for Defending Freedom (ADF), and Jerry Falwell provided the Liberty Counsel with institutional support (Bennett, 2015).

CCLOs have been effective, as witnessed in their advocacy in the *Masterpiece Cakeshop v. Colorado* Civil Rights Commission (2018) case, where the ADF represented the petitioner and bakery owner, Jack Phillips, who was accused of violating state law for denying to make a wedding cake for a same-sex couple. The ADF helped successfully argue before the Supreme Court that the Commission violated Phillips' First Amendment "right to freedom of speech by compelling him to exercise his artistic talents to express a message with which he disagreed and would violate his right to the free exercise of religion" (Vile, 2023). The ADF was also successful in their appeal to the Supreme Court in *Trinity Lutheran Church of Columbia, Inc. v. Comer* (2017), where the Court held that Missouri's denial of the Church's public grant application to purchase rubber playground surface material was a denial of their free exercise rights under the First Amendment because the playground was a public benefit, and the Church was rejected because of its religious status. Furthermore, organizations such as the ADF were also at the forefront of *Dobbs v. Jackson Women's Health Organization* (2022), which overturned a woman's constitutional right to an abortion under *Roe v. Wade* (1973).

There are several keys to CCLO's legal successes. One is that organizations, such as the ADF, create model legislation and pitch it to conservative state legislators to present as bills to pass into law. For example, the ADF created a "model" bill protecting life at fifteen weeks and coordinated with Mississippi's legislature to get it passed into state law. As a result, this abortion ban became the focal point of the *Dobbs* case (Alliance Defending Freedom, 2023). Two, CCLOs also work among each other to coordinate responses within the Christian Legal Movement, particularly with the filing of amicus curiae briefs, which attempt to influence the court's decision. For instance, the American Center for Law and Justice, as well as the Liberty Counsel, each filed amicus briefs in their support of the ADF's appeal in the *Trinity Lutheran Church* case. Third, CCLOs will also coordinate with other organizations in the brief writing process (Dallas, 2017).

According to Ministry Watch, an organization that works to restore credibility to evangelical ministry work by increasing transparency of these groups' activities, there are forty-two Christian legal advocacy organizations with IRS nonprofit status (Ministry Watch, 2023). The Alliance Defending Freedom (ADF), which is focused on in this book due to its involvement in the legislation at the center of the *Dobbs* decision and it is support of the Alliance for Hippocratic Medicine in its legal fight to end the Food and Drug Administration's regulatory authority over emergency contraception, is the third largest revenue grossing CCLO in the country. According to Ministry Watch and these groups' IRS tax filings per ProPublica's Nonprofit Explorer, Table 1.1 lists information about the top ten Christian legal advocacy groups in the country (Ministry Watch, 2023; Suozzo et al., 2023).

As Table 1.1 illustrates, CCLOs are multi-issue organizations that are committed to the values of Christian conservatives, promoted primarily through legal strategies, including filing lawsuits, drafting model legislation, and public education campaigns (Dallas, 2017; Bennett, 2017; Alliance Defending Freedom, 2023). CCLOs are part of the Christian Right and a facet of the Christian Legal Movement. While the Christian Right's activism focuses on political engagement, lobbying, and the election of like-minded candidates, CCLOs provide a specialized legal mechanism that perpetuates the cultural wars, meaning the public divides over topics such as abortion, LGBTQ+ rights, traditional marriage, and religious freedom issues. CCLOs help religious elites frame these issues within a legal context so that even though their positions may not align with most Americans (i.e., as noted above that over 60% of the country believe abortion should be legal in all or most cases) they command political discourse, keeping them at the forefront of policy debates, creating and influencing high-stakes court cases, and capitalizing on division among the public and those in power (Bennett, 2017).

In looking at why social movements, such as the Christian Right and Christian Legal Movement, go to court and organize via various Christian conservative legal organizations (CLLOs), it is important to examine some of the sociolegal scholarship surrounding this question. Some argue that the answer is simple, activist look to the court's coercive power to either uphold legislation or public policy they favor or strike down measures supported or instituted by their opponents. Moreover, legal concepts can be used to frame a movement's grievance and unite activists (Briker, 2023). This framing can be done with legal concepts, such as "right to life" or "religious liberty." Others argue that legal rights can be viewed as "political rights," which are resources used to alter public policy indirectly through increasing movement mobilization, bargaining power, and a sense of collective identity (Scheingold, 1974). On the other hand, some scholars argue legal movements

TABLE 1.1 Top Ten Conservative Christian Legal Organizations in the United States

Rank	*Name*	*Total Revenue*	*President/ CEO*	*Established*	*Headquarters*	*Mission*
1	International Fellowship of Christians and Jews	$219,904,132 (Per 990 available: 2021)	Yael Eckstein	1983	Chicago, IL	Promote understanding and cooperation between Jews and Christians.
2	Able Light	$107,612,471 (Per last 9090 available: 2021)	Keith Jones	1904	Watertown, WI	Christian organization supporting people with intellectual & developmental disabilities.
3	Alliance Defending Freedom	$78,833,050 (Per last 9090 available: 2021)	Kristen Waggoner	1994	Scottsdale, AZ	Protecting religious freedom, free speech, sanctity of life, parental rights, traditional marriage, and family values.
4	The Voices of Martyrs	$77,331,603 (Per last 9090 available: 2020)	Cole Richards	1967	Bartlesville, OK	Serves persecuted Christians around the world.
5	Giving Children Hope	$32,370,795 (Per last 9090 available: 2020)	Pete Bowen	1993	Buena Park, CA	To provide food and health necessities to children and families.

(*Continued*)

TABLE 1.1 (Continued)

Rank	*Name*	*Total Revenue*	*President/ CEO*	*Established*	*Headquarters*	*Mission*
6	American Family Association	$31,046,881 (Per last 9090 available: 2021)	Tim Wildmon	1977	Tupelo, MS	To transform American culture and to give aid to the Church with focus on evangelism, family, morality, sanctity of human life, stewardship, and religious liberty.
7	Faith & Freedom Coalition	$29,681,130 (Per last 9090 available: 2021)	Timothy Head	2009	Duluth, GA	Mobilize effective citizens, speak out in the public area and media on behalf of Christian values.
8	American Center for Law and Justice	$24,492,864 (Per last 9090 available: 2022)	Jay Alan Sekulow	1990	Virginia Beach, VA	Protect religious and constitutional freedoms.
9	Family Research Council	$22,630,464 (Per last 9090 available: 2021)	Tony Perkins	1993	Washington, DC	Advance faith, family, and freedom in public policy and culture from a biblical worldview.
10	Human Coalition	$19,644,890 (Per last 9090 available: 2021)	Jeff Bradford	2009	Plano, TX	End abortion in America.

should be wary of a false sense of hope in securing legal victories, as it can foster backlash by counter movements and activists (Tushnet, 1994). Furthermore, researchers also argue that court victories are "contingent" resources because securing them may spur possible media coverage and further coordination between legal professionals and activists (Briker, 2023). And, even if a group loses a legal battle, it can be beneficial in terms of elevating public consciousness on the issue (McCann, 1994; Bennett, 2017).

It is also important to discuss the American Catholic Church's conservative legal movement alongside the above-noted groups who are largely Evangelical Protestants. As previously mentioned, the pro-life movement, which tends to be dominated by Christian conservatives (Ballard, 2022), was largely made up of Catholics when it first started in the 1960s. In the aftermath of *Roe*, this movement diversified with evangelical and fundamentalist groups joining the ranks (Sabella, 2023). However, the Catholic Church pronounces that from the first century they have been against "the moral evil of every procured abortion" (Catechism of the Catholic Church, 2016). And, in the twentieth century, the Second Vatican Council, in its 1965 *Gaudium Et Spes*, the pastoral constitution on the Church in the modern world, once again affirmed the Church's opposition to abortion. Since the decision in *Roe v. Wade*, the American Catholic Bishops have released dozens of teaching documents on the Church's position against abortion (USCCB, 2023a). Like many religious organizations in the United States, the United States Conference of Catholic Bishops (USCCB), the governing body for the Catholic Church in America, is tax exempt (USCCB, 2023b,c); however, this does not prohibit them from educating the laity or lobbying the government on public policy issues relevant to the faith. The American Catholic Church has long lobbied against abortion and contraception through its Office of Government Relations, which represents the USCCB before Congress (USCCB, 2023d). The USCCB is also active in supporting court cases on public policy issues of concern to the bishops. For example, the USCCB strongly opposed the Department of Health and Human Services' insurance contraception mandate under the Affordable Care Act in 2012 and filed amicus curiae briefs in support of several Catholic University and religious organizations, such as The Little Sisters of the Poor's lawsuits against the Obama Administrations' enforcement of this policy (USCCB, 2023e,f, g). The

USCCB has also supported individuals, religious groups, and even corporations that are not Catholic based, but share the Church's position on these topics. For example, in 2014, the USCCB filed an amicus curiae brief at the Supreme Court of the United States in the support of Hobby Lobby, a closely held company, whose founder, David Greene, an evangelical Christian, successfully argued that the Health and Human Services' contraception mandate on employers violated the 1993 Religious Freedom Restoration Act (SCOTUSblog.com, 2014; USCCB, 2023g). In addition to the USSCB, other Catholic groups, such as the Thomas More Society, a not for profit public interest law firm supporting pro-life issues, traditional family, and religious freedom, as well as the Catholic Bar Association, have been active in their legal advocacy of these issues in both state and federal courts (Thomas More Society, 2023; Catholic Bar Association, 2023).

Dobbs

Over one hundred and forty amicus curiae briefs were filed in the landmark Supreme Court case, *Dobbs v. Jackson Women's Health Organization* (2022), with ninety-one supporting the petitioner, the Mississippi State Department of Health, and fifty-three favoring the respondent, the state's then only abortion clinic (Erskine, 2021). Arguments in these briefs covered a range of issues, such viability standards established in *Roe* and *Casey*, the principle of stare decisis, legislative authority, constitutional philosophy and interpretation, gender equality, medical ethics, fetal personhood, maternal health, reproductive health, the impact on marginalized groups, domestic violence, and the meaning of substantive due process, just to name a few (Erskine, 2021). However, out of all the issues argued, Justice Alito's decision in *Dobbs* focuses on the majority's view that there is no substantive due process liberty securing a woman's constitutional right to an abortion. And, in the words of Associate Justice Clarence Thomas, the concept is "demonstrably erroneous" (p. 2301).

To understand the *Dobbs* decision and how the Court reached its holding, it is important to briefly unpack the controversial concept, substantive due process, along with the *Roe* and *Casey* decisions. The modern concept of substantive due process deals with the interpretation and application of the Fourteenth Amendment. The incorporation clause of this amendment, "…nor shall any state deprive a person of life, liberty, or property, without due process of law….," would start the selective incorporation process by which the Bill of Rights became applicable to the states (Hawley, 2014; Cornell Law School, 2023). In the twentieth century, during the "Lochner era," this clause was used to strike down state laws that were interfering with economic liberty and freedom to contract, both considered fundamental liberties under the Fourteenth Amendment (see *Lochner v. New York,* 1905; Waimber, 2015). The Lochner era ended with the ruling in *West Coast Hotel Co. v. Parrish* (1937), which favored state regulation of minimum wage. However, the concept that certain unenumerated liberties exist and were protected by the Constitution continued and was revisited in landmark cases, such as Griswold *v. Connecticut* (1965) paving the way for *Roe* and *Casey*. In *Griswold*, the Court held that penumbras of privacy exist within the Ninth Amendment, prohibiting states from preventing married couples from using contraception. Some argue that substantive due process was revitalized in this ruling, since the implied right to privacy was held as a fundamental right within the context of the Bill of Rights (Waimber, 2015). Eight years later, *Roe* would accept a similar rationale to strike down a Texas criminal abortion law, which prohibited procuring or attempting an abortion except to save the life of the mother. In *Roe*, the majority agreed with the appellant's argument that the Texas statute criminalizing abortion, improperly invaded individual liberty and privacy, "embodied in the Fourteenth Amendment's due process clause" and is "protected by the Bill of Rights or its penumbras," as held in *Griswold* (p. 715). In addition to announcing a woman's constitutional right to an abortion, *Roe* set up a trimester framework establishing, up to a point of viability, when an individual could terminate their pregnancy with varying levels of state interest. In the case, the Court gave this right a heightened standard of scrutiny from government regulation, but noted that it was not absolute, because at some point (see *Roe* for trimester framework), the state has a sufficiently compelling interest to "sustain regulation" (p. 154). Nineteen years later, *Casey* (1992), a case dealing with restrictive amendments to Pennsylvania's abortion statue, affirmed the essential holding of *Roe*, upholding the substantive "liberty" for a woman to terminate her pregnancy but rejected the trimester framework, replacing it with the undue burden test. The undue burden test essentially held that a woman may elect to end her pregnancy before viability without undue interference from the state. In its plurality opinion, the Court upheld several of Pennsylvania's amendment but stated that spousal notification requirement was unconstitutional.

So, what happened to the view of the Court's abortion rulings was "precedent on precedent" (Sneed, 2021)? Well, what happened was a long game strategy employed by the Christian Right and CCLO, as evidenced by the legal advocacy of the Alliance Defending Freedom. In 2018, Becky Currie, a registered nurse and Republican Representative for Mississippi's House of Representatives, introduced the Gestational Age Act, based on a model bill crafted by the ADF in 2017. This bill protected life at fifteen weeks of pregnancy to satisfy three compelling state interests: protecting the life of the unborn, advancing women's health, and upholding the integrity of medical professionals in Mississippi (Alliance Defending Freedom, 2023). The bill prohibited abortions in the state except in times of medical emergency or severe fetal abnormality (*Dobbs v. Jackson Women's Health Organization*, 2022). The bill argued that at fifteen weeks of pregnancy, fetuses have heartbeats, engage in physical movement, such as kicking, opening and closing fingers, hiccupping, and can likely feel pain. The law also noted possible medical risk posed to mothers after this gestational period. On March 19, 2018, Governor Phil Bryant signed the legislation into law, and shortly thereafter, Mississippi's only abortion clinic, Jackson Women's Health Organization, sued the state (Alliance Defending Freedom, 2023). The US District Court for the Southern District of Mississippi granted the plaintiffs' summary judgment motion and enjoined the legislation in all applications. The US Court of Appeals for the Fifth Circuit affirmed (*Dobbs v. Jackson Women's Health Organization*, 2022). Subsequently, the state petitioned the Supreme Court to hear the case. With the Court's conservative majority, due to Trump's three appointments: Neil Gorsuch, Brett Kavanaugh, and Amey Coney Barnett, the state felt confident in its position (Liptak, 2021). During this time, the ADF's appellate division worked with Mississippi's legal team to prepare their argument before the Court, and on June 24, 2022, *Roe v. Wade* was overturned. Essentially, the Supreme Court held that the Constitution does not provide a right to abortion and that the authority to regulate such an activity is up to each state and its elective representatives (Alliance Defending Freedom, 2023; *Dobbs v. Jackson Women's Health Organization,* 2022).

The New Legal Battles in a Post-*Dobbs* America

The *Dobbs* decision will undoubtedly impact constitutional interpretation for decades to come, as the current Court calls into question protections for unenumerated rights in the Constitution. This landmark decision was not only celebrated among Christian conservatives and their affiliated legal movements but also provided these groups with additional momentum to take up other legal battles against abortion. These groups are keenly aware that though *Dobbs* returned the decision on abortion to the states, it did not prohibit them from electing to keep the right to terminate a pregnancy on the table. Therefore, CCLOs, such as the Alliance Defending Freedom and other groups, like the Alliance for Hippocratic Medicine, have taken up a new charge in their effort to eliminate abortion in America, the fight over emergency contraception.

The purpose of this book is to evaluate where the American legal and political system is in the aftermath of the *Dobbs* decision. With the overturning of *Roe*, both conservative and liberal states have doubled down on their efforts to either restrict or expand access to reproductive services. In the absence of constitutional protections, abortion policies are decided at the state level, creating a hodgepodge framework and fueling legal and political battles ahead of and even after the 2024 General Election. The subsequent chapters navigate this fluid dynamic and its impact on the country by focusing on regulatory efforts to restrict the use of medicated abortion and the measures conservative and liberal states are taking to either curtail or expand reproductive rights in their respective jurisdictions.

Specifically, Chapter 2 continues to look at the role of CCLOs and their desire to eliminate nearly all types of abortion in the United States. This is done by examining the case of the *Alliance for Hippocratic Medicine (AHM) et al. v. U.S. Food and Drug Administration* (2023). The AHM, with the help of the Alliance Defending Freedom and other groups, like the Christian Legal Society, filed a lawsuit over the FDA's two decade old approval of mifepristone, which, when used with misoprostol, works to formulate an abortion pill, one of the most common methods of terminating a pregnancy in the United States. The AHM and ADF argue that the FDA abused its authority when it approved mifepristone in 2000 through an accelerated process. This chapter evaluates the legal arguments of the AHM and Biden Administration via the FDA and examines how Christian-based interest groups, such as the ADF, continue their legal strategy to push and ramp up their pro-life agenda.

In a post-*Dobbs* America, the divide between "Red" (conservative/Republican) and "Blue" (liberal/Democratic) states has become more prominent, and the stakes surrounding reproductive rights have grown higher. With the aid of theories of how the dynamics of activism can influence policy outcomes, Chapter 3 evaluates the current differences between "Red" and "Blue" states on abortion rights in this era (Yamane and Oldmixon, 2006; Layman and Weaver, 2016; Gonzalez, 2023). This chapter employs a qualitative analysis, examining which states protect access to abortion via state law, ballot initiatives, state constitution, executive orders, or a State Supreme Court precedent versus states that have utilized the legislature or courts to limit or completely deny access (Gonzalez, 2023). This analysis will also uncover the political and religious influences behind these state policies and how they further create a sense of tension on the abortion issue across the country's federal system of government (Reingold et al., 2021).

Chapter 3 gives an overview of where the United States is on abortion and its impact in upcoming elections. This chapter discusses how religious as well as progressive groups continue to influence the political process to get public policies on abortion implemented according to their views. This section concludes this book with a discussion on the Supreme Court's ruling on the FDA's authorization of mifepristone and what implications this decision has on the future of abortion access across the country. Overall, this chapter highlights how the issue of abortion underscores the point that elections matter and have long-term consequences.

Finally, Chapter 5 discusses the abortion issue factored into the 2024 Presidential Election. This chapter analyzes how the American people not only voted overwhelmingly for Donald Trump but also supported key state initiatives that protected abortion access. This chapter also evaluates key cabinet positions in the new Trump Administration, and how it will impact the status of abortion over the next four years. Overall, this chapter highlights how the issue of abortion underscores the point that elections matter and have long-term consequences.

References

Abington School District v. Schempp, 374 U.S. 203 (1963)

Adams, G. (1997) 'Abortion: Evidence of an Issue Evolution', *American Journal of Political Science*, 41(3), pp.718–737. Available at: https://doi.org/10.2307/2111673 (Accessed: 19 July 2023).

Alliance Defending Freedom (2023) *What You May Not Know: How ADF Helped Overturn Roe v. Wade*. Available at: https://adflegal.org/article/what-you-may-not-know-how-adf-helped-overturn-roe-v-wade (Accessed: 19 July 2023).

Baker, C.N., Fried, M.G., Kaplan, L., Yanow, S., Cupaiuolo, C. (2022) 'The History of Abortion Law in the United States', *Our Bodies Ourselves Today at Suffolk University*. Available at: https://www.ourbodiesourselves.org/health-info/u-s-abortion-history/ (Accessed: 29 June 2023).

Balkin, J.M. (2024) 'Abortion, Partisan Entrenchment, and the Republican Party', in L.B. Bollinger and G.R. Stone (eds.) *Roe v. Dobbs: The Past, Present, and Future of a Constitutional Right to Abortion*. New York: Oxford University Press. pp. 81–100.

Ballard, J. (2022) 'Which Religious Groups' Members are Most Likely to Identify as Pro-Choice?', *YouGov*. Available at: https://today.yougov.com/topics/politics/articles-reports/2022/05/13/which-religious-groups-members-abortion-poll (Accessed: 19 July 2023).

Bennett, D. (2015) 'The Rise of Christian Conservative Legal Organizations', *Religion & Politics*. Available at: https://religionandpolitics.org/2015/06/10/the-rise-of-christian-conservative-legal-organizations/ (Accessed: 19 July 2023).

Bennet, D. (2017) *Defending Faith: The Politics of the Christian Conservative Legal Movement*. Lawrence, KY: University Press of Kansas.

Bob Jones *University v. United States*, 461 U.S. 574 (1983).

Briker, G. (2023) 'The Anatomy of Social Movement Litigation,' *The Yale Law Journal,* 132(7), pp.2304–2359. Available at: https://www.yalelawjournal.org/note/the-anatomy-of-social-movement-litigation (Accessed: 19 July 2023).

Brown v. *Board of Education of Topeka*, 347 U.S. 483 (1954)

Catechism of the Catholic Church (2016) *Life in Christ Part Three: 2322*. Available at: https://www.usccb.org/sites/default/files/flipbooks/catechism/560/ (Accessed: 06 June 2023).

Catholic Bar Association (2023) *Mission of the Catholic Bar Association*. Available at: https://catholicbar.org/Mission-and-Purpose (Accessed: 20 July 2023).

Claassen, R.L. (2018) 'Understanding the Political Motivations of Evangelical Voters', in P.A. Djupe and R.L. Claassen (eds.) *The Evangelical Crackup? The Future of the Evangelical-Republican Coalition*. Philadelphia, PA: Temple University Press. pp. 49–62.

Cole Smith, W. (2023) '30 Largest Christian Advocacy Organizations', *Ministry Watch*. Available at: https://ministrywatch.com/30-largest-christian-advocacy-organizations/ (Accessed: 18 July 2023).

Conger, K.H. (2018) 'Rethinking the State-Level Strategy: The Christian Right and Left in the States', in P.A. Djupe and R.L. Claassen (eds.) *The Evangelical Crackup? The Future of the Evangelical-Republican Coalition*. Philadelphia, PA: Temple University Press. pp. 94–108.

Cornell Law School (2023) *The Fourteenth Amendment*. Available at: https://www.law.cornell.edu/constitution/amendmentxiv (Accessed: 09 August 2023).

Dallas, K. (2017) 'Serving God by Suing Others: Inside the Christian Conservative Legal Movement', *National Catholic Reporter*, 5 August. Available at: https://www.ncronline.org/news/serving-god-suing-others-inside-christian-conservative-legal-movement (Accessed: 19 July 2023).

de Vogue, A., Sneed, T., and Cole, D. (2023) 'Supreme Court Issues Report on Dobbs Leak But Says it Hasn't Identified the Leaker', *CNN*, 19 January. Available at: https://www.cnn.com/2023/01/19/politics/supreme-court-dobbs-report-leak/index.html#:~:text=The%20leak%20–%20the%20worst%20breach,a%20constitutional%20right%20to%20abortion (Accessed: 21 June 2023).

Dobbs v. Jackson Women's Health Organization, 142 S.Ct. 2228 (2022)

Erskine, E. (2021) 'We Read all the Amicus Briefs in Dobbs So You Don't Have To', *SCOTUSblog*, 30 November. Available at: https://www.scotusblog.com/2021/11/we-read-all-the-amicus-briefs-in-dobbs-so-you-dont-have-to/#:~:text=More%20than%20140%20amicus%20briefs,from%20across%20the%20ideological%20spectrum (Accessed: 20 July 2023).

Engel v. Vitale, 370 U.S. 421 (1962)

Fisher, M. (2012) 'GOP Platform Through the Years Shows the Party's Shift from Moderate to Conservative', *The Washington Post*, 28 August. Available at: https://www.washingtonpost.com/politics/gop-platform-through-the-years-shows-partys-shift-from-moderate-to-conservative/2012/08/28/09094512-ed70-11e1-b09d-07d971dee30a_story.html (Accessed: 29 June 2023).

Foster, J.C. (2009) 'Scope Monkey Trial', in J. Seigenthaler (ed.) *The First Amendment Encyclopedia*. Middle Tennessee State University: Free Speech Center. Available at https://www.mtsu.edu/first-amendment/article/1100/scopes-monkey-trial (Accessed: 21 June 2023).

Gonzalez, O. (2023) 'Where Abortion Has Been Banned Now That Roe v. Wade is Overturned', *AXIOS*, 23 August. Available at: https://www.axios.com/2022/06/25/abortion-illegal-7-states-more-bans-coming (Accessed: 10 August 2023).

Green, E. (2022) 'How the Federalist Society Won', *The New Yorker*, 24 July. Availableat:https://www.newyorker.com/news/annals-of-education/how-the-federalist-society-won (Accessed: 18 October 2024).

Greenhouse, L., and Siegal, R.B. (2011) 'Before (and After) Roe v. Wade: New Questions About Backlash', *The Yale Law Journal*, 120(8), pp.2028–2087. Available at https://www.jstor.org/stable/41149586 (Accessed: 21 June 2023).

Griswold v. Connecticut, 381 U.S. 479 (1965)

Hawley, Joshua D. (2014) 'The Intellectual Origins of (Modern) Substantive Due Process', *Texas Law Review*, 93, pp.275–350. Available at https://scholarship.law.missouri.edu/facpubs/525/ (Accessed: 21 June 2023).

Howe, A. (2023) 'Supreme Court Investigators Fail to Identify Who Leaked Dobbs Opinion', *SCOTUSblog*, 19 January. Available at: https://www.scotusblog.com/2023/01/supreme-court-investigators-fail-to-identify-who-leaked-dobbs-opinion/#:~:text=The%20leaked%20opinion%20sparked%20protests,to%20take%20extra%20security%20precautions (Accessed: 21 June 2023).

Kroll, A., Bernstein, A., and Marritz, I. (2023) 'We Don't Talk About Leonard: The Man Behind the Right's Supreme Court Supermajority', *Propublica*, 11 October. Available at: https://www.propublica.org/article/we-dont-talk-about-leonard-leo-supreme-court-supermajority (Accessed: 18 October 2024).

Layman, G.C., and Weaver, C.L. (2016) 'Religion and Secularism Among American Party Activists', *Politics and Religion,* 9(2), pp.271–295. Available at: https://doi.org/10.1017/S1755048316000079

Lewis, A. (2017) *The Rights Turn in Conservative Christian Politics: How Abortion Transformed the Culture Wars*. United Kingdom: Cambridge University Press.

Liptak, A. (2018) 'The Threat to Roe v. Wade in the Case of the Missing Precedent', *The New York Times*, 17 September. Available at: https://www.nytimes.com/2018/09/17/us/politics/kavanaugh-abortion-precedent.html (Accessed: 21 June 2023).

Liptak, A. (2021) 'Supreme Court Seems Poised to Uphold Mississippi's Abortion Law,' *The New York Times*, 1 December. Available at: https://www.nytimes.com/2021/12/01/us/politics/supreme-court-mississippi-abortion-law.html (Accessed: 09 August 2023).

Lochner v. New York, 198 U.S. 45 (1905)

Masterpiece Cakeshop, Ltd. v. Colorado Civil Rights Com'n, 138 S.Ct. 1719 (2018)

McCann, M.W. (1994) *Rights at Work: Pay Equity Reform and the Politics of Legal Mobilization*. Chicago: The University of Chicago Press.

Ministry Watch (2023) *Compare Ministries: Advocacy*. Available at: https://db.ministrywatch.com/compare.php?sector=Advocacy (Accessed: 19 July 2023).

National Association for the Repeal of Abortion Laws (2023) *About Us*. Available at: https://www.prochoiceamerica.org/about/ (Accessed: 29 June 2023).

National Right to Life Committee (2023) *History of National Right to Life*. Available at: https://www.nrlc.org/about/history/ (Accessed: 29 June 2023).

Nixon Presidential Library (2022) *The Equal Rights Amendment*. Available at: https://www.nixonlibrary.gov/news/equal-rights-amendment#:~:text=The%20Equal%20Rights%20Amendment%20(ERA,longer%20be%20determined%20by%20gender. (Accessed: 29 June 2023).

Payne, B.J. (2023) 'Religious Right – Timeline Movement', *The Association of Religion Data Archives*. Available at: https://www.thearda.com/us-religion/history/timelines/entry?etype=3&eid=17 (Accessed: 21 June 2023).

Pew Research Center (2022) *Majority of Public Disapproves of Supreme Court's Decision to Overturn Roe v. Wade*. Available at: https://www.pewresearch.org/politics/2022/07/06/majority-of-public-disapproves-of-supreme-courts-decision-to-overturn-roe-v-wade/ (Accessed: 1 June 2023).

Planned Parenthood of Southeastern Pennsylvania v. Casey, 505 U.S. 833 (1992)

Reingold, B., Kreitzer, R., and Swers, M. (2021) 'Anti-Abortion Policymaking and Women's Representation', *Political Research Quarterly*, 74(2), pp.403–420. Available at: https://doi.org/10.1177/1065912920903381

Roe v. Wade, 410 U.S. 113 (1973)

Ruby, R. (2007) 'A Christian Right Without Falwell', *Pew Research Center*, 16 May. Available at: https://www.pewresearch.org/religion/2007/05/16/a-christian-right-without-falwell/ (Accessed: 18 July 23).

Sabella, J.L. (2023) 'Pro-Life and Rescue Movements-Timeline Movement', *The Association of Religion Data Archives*. Available at: https://www.thearda.com/us-religion/history/timelines/entry?etype=3&eid=31 (Accessed: 19 July 2023).

Scanlon, K. (2023) 'How the Catholic Church Influenced the Pro-Life Movement Before and After Roe', *Catholic Review*, 9 January. Available at: https://catholicreview.org/how-the-catholic-church-influenced-the-pro-life-movement-before-and-after-roe/ (Accessed: 21 June 2023).

Scheingold, S. (1974) *The Politics of Rights: Lawyers, Public Policy, and Political Change*. New Haven, CT: Yale University Press.

SCOTUSblog (2014) *Burwell v. Hobby Lobby Stores, Inc*. Available at: https://www.scotusblog.com/case-files/cases/sebelius-v-hobby-lobby-stores-inc/ (Accessed: 20 July 2023).

Sneed, T. (2021) 'Brett Kavanuagh, Who Touted Importance of Precedent During Confirmation Fight, Downplays it as He Considers Reversing Roe', *CNN*, 2 December. Available at: https://www.cnn.com/2021/12/01/politics/kavanaugh-abortion-precedent-roe-mississippi/index.html (Accessed: 09 August 2023).

Stewart, K. (2022) 'How the Christian Right Took Over the Judiciary and Changed America', *The Guardian*, 17 September. Available at: https://

www.theguardian.com/world/2022/jun/25/roe-v-wade-abortion-christian-right-america (Accessed: 4 October 2024).

Suozzo, A., Schwencke, K., Tigas, M., Wei, S., Glassford, A., and Roberts, B. (2023) 'Nonprofit Explorer Research Tax-Exempt Organizations,' *ProPublica*. Available at: https://projects.propublica.org/nonprofits/ (Accessed: 19 July 2023).

The Federalist Society (2024) *About Us*. Available at: https://fedsoc.org/about-us (Accessed: 18 October 2024).

The Heritage Foundation (2024) *Judicial Appointment Tracker*. Available at: https://www.heritage.org/judicialtracker (Accessed: 18 October 2024).

Thomas More Society (2023) *History: Forged in the Crucible of Courtroom Conflict*. Available at: https://www.thomasmoresociety.org/history (Available 20 July 2023).

Trinity Lutheran Church of Columbia, Inc. v. Comer, 582 U.S. 449 (2017)

Tushnet, G. (1994) 'The Critique of Rights', *Southern Methodist Law Review*, 47(1), pp.23–34. Available at https://scholar.smu.edu/smulr/vol47/iss1/6/.

USCCB (2023a) *Roe v. Wade*. Available at: https://www.usccb.org/issues-and-action/human-life-and-dignity/abortion/roe-v-wade (Accessed: 20 July 2023).

USCCB (2023b) *About Us*. Available at: https://www.usccb.org/about (Accessed: 20 July 2023).

USCCB (2023c) *General Counsel: Tax and Group Ruling*. Available at: https://www.usccb.org/offices/general-counsel/tax-and-group-ruling (Accessed: 20 July 2023).

USCCB (2023d) *Office of Government Relations*. Available at: https://www.usccb.org/offices/government-relations (Accessed: 20 July 2023).

USCCB (2023e) March 14 *Statement on Religious Freedom and HHS Mandate*. Available at: https://www.usccb.org/committees/religious-liberty/march-14-statement-religious-freedom-and-hhs-mandate (Accessed: 20 July 2023).

USCCB (2023f) *The Little Sisters of the Poor and the HHS Mandate*. Available at: https://www.usccb.org/committees/religious-liberty/little-sisters-poor-and-hhs-mandate. (Accessed: 20 July 2023).

USCCB (2023g) *Amicus Briefs*. Available at: https://www.usccb.org/offices/general-counsel/amicus-briefs (Accessed: 20. July 2023).

Vatican (1965) *Pastoral Constitution on the Church in the Modern World: Gaudium Et Spes*. Available at: https://www.vatican.va/archive/hist_councils/ii_vatican_council/documents/vat-ii_const_19651207_gaudium-et-spes_en.html (Accessed: 20 July 2023).

Vile, J.R. (2023) 'Masterpiece Cakeshop v. Colorado Civil Rights Commission (2018)', *Free Speech Center*. 12 August. Available at: https://firstamendment.mtsu.edu/article/masterpiece-cakeshop-v-colorado-civil-rights-commission/#:~:text=A%20state%20

Administrative%20Law%20Judge,Amendment%20rights%20to%20the%20free (Accessed: 17 May 2024).

Waimber, J. (2015) 'Lochner v. New York: Fundamental Rights and Economic Liberty', *The Constitution Center*, 26 October. Available at: https://constitutioncenter.org/blog/lochner-v-new-york-fundamental-rights-and-economic-liberty (Accessed: 09 August 2023).

West Coast Hotel Co. v. Parrish, 300 U.S. 379 (1937)

Wilcox, C. (1988) 'The Christian Right in Twentieth Century America: Continuity and Change', *The Review of Politics*, 50(4), pp.659–681. Available at: https://www.jstor.org/stable/1407358.

Yamane, D., and Oldmixon, E.A. (2006) 'Religion in the Legislative Arena: Affiliation, Salience, Advocacy, and Public Policymaking', *Legislative Studies Quarterly*, 31(3), pp.433–460. Available at: https://www.jstor.org/stable/40263394.

2

PRO-LIFE RELIGIOUS INTEREST GROUPS AND THE REGULATORY AUTHORITY OVER REPRODUCTIVE RIGHTS

On Tuesday, November 8, 2022, the day of the midterm election, the backlash against the Biden Administration, dubbed the "red wave" by political analysts, did not hit the shores of voting precincts, despite the President's approval rating hovering around 40% (Cillizza, 2022). Voters in critical states, like Michigan and Pennsylvania, ranked *abortion*, not inflation or crime, as the most important issue of the election. And though they lost the House of Representatives, Democrats gained a seat in the Senate, held onto several governorships, took away two legislative chambers from Republicans in Michigan and Minnesota, and gained complete control of state capitols in Maryland and Massachusetts (Schneider and Otterbein, 2022). It was clear that in the wake of the *Dobbs* decision, abortion was a top electoral issue, especially for women, where a gender gap emerged, suggesting both younger and older women favored Democratic candidates (Kurtzleben, 2022). For example, in the weeks following the landmark *Dobbs* decision, more than 70% of newly registered voters in Kansas were female. Though percentages vary, this emerging pattern continued with an increase of female voter registration numbers across multiple states, such as Pennsylvania, Ohio, Oklahoma, Florida, North Carolina, Idaho, Alabama, New Mexico, and Maine, which worked to the advantage of Democrats (Paris and Cohn, 2022).

Yet, despite election results showing that 61% of Americans believe abortion should be legal, the Christian Legal Movement took

DOI: 10.4324/9781032636177-2

the opportunity to launch another attack on reproductive rights by targeting the Food and Drug Administration's (FDA) regulatory authority over the abortion pill (Hartig, 2022). Just days after the midterm election, the Alliance for Hippocratic Medicine (AHM) filed a lawsuit against the executive regulatory agency in the US District Court for the Northern District of Texas, located in Amarillo (NARAL, 2023). In the lawsuit, the AHM looked the court to revoke the FDA's approval of mifepristone, a drug that blocks the needed hormone progesterone to sustain a pregnancy, which is used in a regimen with misoprostol to form the "abortion pill." This regimen is used to terminate pregnancy that is less than seventy days in duration (Mayo Clinic, 2023; FDA, 2023). In the complaint, the AHM, represented by the Christian Conservative Legal Organization (CCLO), Alliance Defending Freedom (ADF) questioned the FDA's accelerated approval of chemical abortion drugs, which the plaintiffs argue the agency could only do by labeling pregnancy an "illness." The AHM argued that the pregnancy is not an "illness" or "serious" nor "life-threatening" condition and the FDA's decision was political, not scientific (*Alliance for Hippocratic Medicine v. U.S. Food and Drug Administration,* 2022, p. 2).

However, before delving further into the AHM's and Biden Administration's arguments over the FDA's regulatory authority on chemical abortion, it is important to first take a closer look at who the AHM is, why it was established in Amarillo, TX, and filed its original complaint with the Northern District Court.

The Alliance for Hippocratic Medicine

The AHM is an interest group of pro-life medical professionals. The AHM consists of seven partnering organizations: the Catholic Medical Association, the Coptic Medical Association, the American Association of Pro-Life Obstetricians and Gynecologists (AAPLOG), the Christian and Dental Association, the American College of Pediatricians, the National Association of Prolife Nurses, and the American College of Family Medicine (The Alliance for Hippocratic Medicine, 2023a). The AHM is incorporated in Tennessee as a nonprofit organization, but as of August 5, 2022, they registered an agency in Amarillo, Texas, just three months before they filed their lawsuit against the FDA (Hammonds, 2023). The AHM's mission is to "uphold and promote the fundamental principles of Hippocratic medicine," which includes "protecting the vulnerable at the beginning and end of life." Although the AHM's presence is relatively new in Texas, members of this organization have been challenging the FDA's approval of the abortion pill since August 2002 (Alliance for Hippocratic Medicine, 2023b). In March 2016, the FDA denied the citizen petition filed by these members. During the COVID pandemic, the FDA loosened some regulations on the abortion pill by temporarily removing the in-person dispensing requirement, and in December 2021, the FDA denied another citizen petition by members of the AHM. Subsequently, the FDA permanently removed the in-person dispensing requirement, opening the opportunity for the abortion pill to be accessible via telemedicine and mail (The Alliance for Hippocratic Medicine , 2023b). Some argue these developments, along with the appointment of the Honorable Judge Matthew Kacsmaryk to the US District Court for the Northern District of Texas, are what spurred the AHM to relocate to Amarillo and file suit there (NARAL, 2023).

Forum and Judge Shopping

In the last several years, federal courts have seen cases challenging a variety of government actions. Plaintiffs in these cases often look for flexibility in selecting the court to file their case. Acting as strategic actors, plaintiffs sometimes calculate where to file their suit based on their perception of how certain legal rules in a jurisdiction may or may not favorably apply to their claims (Lampe, 2022). This practice is known as "forum shopping." Though forum shopping is limited in the federal court system by things such as the *Erie Doctrine*, which holds that a federal court sitting in diversity jurisdiction must apply the substantive law of the state in which it sits, it still can occur (Cornell Law School, 2023). Additionally, some parties may also try to bring their claim before a specific judge, a practice known as "judge shopping" (Lampe, 2022).

Keeping the above in mind, we can now assess a plausible reason or argument for why the AHM filed its suit against the FDA in the US District Court for the Northern District of Texas. First, it is important to understand that the claim the AHM filed with the court is regarding a question over the FDA's regulatory authority, which is a matter of federal question jurisdiction. There are two main factors that determine where a claim can proceed: jurisdiction and venue. Jurisdiction deals with the power of a court to rule on a case. For a court to have the authority over a case, it must have personal jurisdiction over the parties and subject matter jurisdiction, meaning it can decide on the legal issues presented. Federal courts have both diversity and subject matter jurisdiction. Subject matter jurisdiction deals with the court being able to hear a specific type of claim. In the case of the AHM against the FDA, the plaintiff's claim deals with a federal question, therefore, it was appropriate for a federal district court to hear the case (Lampe, 2022).

Now, why did the AHM choose to file their suit in the district court in Amarillo, Texas? The answer lies in the issue of venue, again, this refers to the court location where it is proper for a case to proceed. Venue will occur in a court close to the geographic area where one or more of the parties are located (Lampe, 2022). As discussed above, the AHM registered itself in Amarillo, Texas, just three months before it filed its suit against the FDA; therefore, the Northern District of Texas was the appropriate venue for the case (Hammonds, 2023). However, there is the argument that judge shopping was also part of the AHM's legal strategy. For instance, there are ninety-four federal district courts throughout the United States, with each district divided into divisions. In Texas, there are four federal district courts with twenty-seven divisions. Eight of these divisions only have one judge; therefore, any case filed in these respective divisions will automatically go to that one judge, so parties are aware of who will preside over their case. Judge Matthew Kacsmaryk, a Trump appointee, is the only federal judge in the Amarillo division of the US District Court for the Northern District of Texas (Chemerinsky, 2023). Judge Kacsmaryk is a former lawyer who served as Deputy General Counsel for First Liberty Institute and Assistant US Attorney for the Northern District of Texas (The Federalist Society, 2023). The First Liberty Institute is a Christian Conservative Legal Organization dedicated to defending religious freedom (First Liberty Institute, 2023). Some, such as legal scholar Erwin Chemerinsky, argue that the AHM's move to file in this division was intentional because, "Conservative litigators know if they file their case in federal court in Amarillo, their judge will be Kacsmaryk" (Chemerinsky, 2023).

So, beyond Kacsmaryk being a judicial nominee by a president who promised to appoint "pro-life" judges to the federal judiciary, what other factors could've led the AHM to "shop" for this judge when filing their case against the FDA (NBC News, 2016)? Well, some point to Kacsmaryk's family history as a factor. According to the *Washington Post*, when Kacsmaryk was a young law student, his seventeen-year-old sister gave birth to his nephew at a maternity center. Kacsmaryk traveled to see his nephew at the center before he was given up for adoption. Kacsmaryk later became a board member of Christian Homes and Family Services, the organization that took in his sister when she chose adoption over abortion (2023). Although judicial officers are supposed to be independent and impartial, some argue that Judge Kacsmaryk's conservative background may have pushed the AHM to hedge their bets when filing their suit in Amarillo, where he was sure to get the case. For example, Wheeler (2023a) notes that key Biden Administration cases involving immigration, reproductive health, and LGBTQ rights have all been before Judge Kacsmaryk and hit roadblocks, as seen in his decision to halt federal protection for asylum seekers, eliminating rules expanding teen access to birth control, as well as rejecting a policy that stopped doctors from discrimination against patients based on their gender identity or sexual orientation.

Since the *Alliance for Hippocratic Medicine v. U.S.* Food and Drug Administration (2023) was filed in the Northern District of Texas, the federal Judicial Conference, the judiciary's administrative unit, has approved a new policy to combat forum shopping. As discussed above, this issue has come up with particular attention to federal districts in Texas, where one judge is automatically assigned cases and interest groups file their petitions there in the hope of getting a decision in their favor based on the judicial officers' ideological background. On March 12, 2024, the Conference stated that a civil claim looking to bar or implement a state or federal action would now be randomly assigned to judges throughout federal judicial districts and that the policy overrides local orders allowing for only one judge to hear all cases filed at their courthouse. The policy change comes as claims for national injunctions are on the rise (Wheeler, 2024). However, US Senate Republican leaders, such as Senators Mitch McConnell (Republican from Kentucky), John Cornyn (Republican from Texas), and Thom Tillis (Republican from North Carolina) stated in a March 14, 2024 letter, directed to the chief judges of US District Courts throughout the country, that the Conference's policy was not legislation and therefore, it was not up to this body but Congress to decide how cases should be assigned to lower courts (Monyah and Wheeler, 2024). This move by the Conference and rebuke by Republican leaders will keep forum shopping a contested issues as the interest groups and government officials keep navigating the court system in filing their claims.

The Arguments by the Alliance for Hippocratic Medicine

Now that the parties and selection of where the AHM's case against the FDA was originally heard have been discussed, it is important to look at the arguments and case timeline.

Starting with the plaintiffs, the AHM, made several key arguments in their original complaint relating to their position that the US FDA "chose politics over science," by failing to live up to its mission of protecting the health, safety, and welfare of Americans by rejecting or limiting the use of dangerous drugs, like mifepristone (*Alliance for Hippocratic Medicine v. U.S. Food and Drug Administration,* 2022, p. 2). The AHM argued for a preliminary and permanent injunction ordering the FDA to withdraw mifepristone and misoprostol as an approved form of chemical abortion (*Alliance for Hippocratic Medicine v. U.S. Food and Drug Administration,* 2022, pp. 110–111).

Again, mifepristone is a drug that blocks the hormone progesterone, which is needed to sustain pregnancy. Mifepristone, when used with misoprostol, a medication prescribed to prevent stomach ulcers, can end pregnancy within seventy days or less since the first day of a woman's last menstrual period (FDA, 2023a). This drug combination works by the mifepristone causing the embryo to separate from the uterine lining, while the misoprostol induces abortion by causing contractions and expelling the embryo (National Library of Medicine, 2024). The AHM argues the process to make chemical abortion accessible in the United States began under the Clinton Administration when they encouraged the French manufacturer of the abortion pill, RU-486, to donate their patent rights to a nonprofit group, the Population Council (*Alliance for Hippocratic Medicine v. U.S. Food and Drug Administration*, 2022, p. 2). News outlets during this time noted the unconventional approach taken by the Clinton Administration to work around obstacles, so that RU-486 could be available for use in the United States, since it was banned by the previous President, George H.W. Bush. As a result, in 1992, manufacturers of the RU-486 refused to market the drug in the United States; however, this began to change a year later under the Clinton Administration (Harvard Library, 2001). In their complaint, the AHM argues that after Population Council received the patent rights to mifepristone, they submitted a new drug application for chemical abortion and worked alongside the FDA during the drug's review process, which was approved in 2000. The AHM claims this process was rushed, arguing that in order to approve the chemical abortion drug, the FDA had to look to the Code of Federal Regulations, § 314 Subpart H, which gives the agency the ability to grant an "accelerated approval" of "certain new drug products that have been studied for their safety and effectiveness in treating serious or life threatening illnesses and that provide meaningful therapeutic benefit to patients over existing treatments."

However, the AHM states that pregnancy is not a life-threatening illness and it "rarely leads to complications that threaten the life of the mother or child" (*Alliance for Hippocratic Medicine v. U.S. Food and Drug Administration*, 2022, p. 15). The AHM further argues that the FDA has increased the gestational age for which pregnant women or adolescents can take the chemical abortion drug from seven to ten weeks, despite claims that increased risk is involved in doing so. The AHM also finds it problematic that in 2016, the FDA changed the dosage for chemical abortion, decreased the required number of in-person office visits from three to one, expanded who could prescribe the drugs, and discontinued the requirement of abortion providers to report non-fatal complications from chemical abortion drugs. Furthermore, the AHM argued that in 2019, the FDA approved a generic of mifepristone without imposing up-to-date clinic investigations on this new version, skirting requirements under the Federal Food, Drug, and Cosmetic Act, as well as the Pediatric Research and Equity Act (*Alliance for Hippocratic Medicine v. U.S. Food and Drug Administration,* 2022, pp. 3–5).

Another point of interest the AHM raised in its original complaint to the District Court in Amarillo is that the chemical abortion regimen has adverse health effects. The AHM claims that by blocking a woman's progesterone receptors in the uterus, which is necessary for the growth of a fetus, mifepristone begins to block the natural hormone and "chemically destroys the baby's environment in the uterus, blocks nutrition to the baby, and ultimately starves the baby to death in the mother's womb" (*Alliance for Hippocratic Medicine v. U.S. Food and Drug Administration*, 2022, p. 17). And, because mifepristone alone only works about 25% of the time to terminate pregnancy, the AHM argues that the FDA's chemical drug abortion regimen calls for the use of misoprostol, which induces cramps and contractions "in an attempt to expel the baby from the mother's womb" (*Alliance for Hippocratic Medicine v. U.S. Food and Drug Administration,* 2022, p. 18) Furthermore, the FDA argues under this regimen 10% of women need follow up medical treatment for incomplete or failed chemical abortion attempts, with over a third requiring surgery if the drugs are taken in the second trimesters (*Alliance for Hippocratic Medicine v. U.S.* F*ood and Drug Administration,* 2022, p. 18) Essentially, the AHM argues that chemical abortion is not safer than surgical abortion, as they claim 20% of females will have adverse effects after taking chemical abortion pills and that the regime increases abortion-related emergency room visits. The AHM also addresses potentially adverse mental health effects for undergoing chemical abortion ((*Alliance for Hippocratic Medicine v. U.S. Food and Drug Administration,* 2022, p. 21).

Furthermore, the AHM complaint argues against the FDA's 2021 "Non-Enforcement Decision" on mifepristone, which stopped the agency from requiring abortion practitioners to provide in-person dispensing of the drug and allowed for mail-order prescriptions of the chemical abortion pill. The FDA argued that this action was taken because of the COVID-19 public health emergency; however, the AHM argues this was a way to circumvent safety protocols and further relax the conditions under which the drug is prescribed. In December of 2021, two and half years after the AHM filed a citizens petition requesting the FDA restore the pre-2016 conditions to the drug regimen, the agency rejected their request, and the Biden Administration announced it would permanently allow the chemical abortion pill to be sent via mail (*Id.* at pp.5–6).

Ultimately, the AHM's complaint centers around their effort to stop the increased access to abortion that the chemical abortion pill provides, particularly because it no longer requires multiple doctor visits and has been approved to be distributed via mail by the FDA since December 2021. This goal is evidenced via the points in their complaint noted above and the argument that easy access to chemical abortion pills aids sex traffickers and abusers because their victims do not have to enter an actual facility to undergo termination of their pregnancy, but instead can be forced to take the medication without this step. As a result, their abuse is not detected by professionals trained to identify and assist victims of sex trafficking (*Alliance for Hippocratic Medicine v. U.S. Food and Drug Administration,* 2022, p. 6).

The FDA's Opposition to AHM's Motion for a Preliminary Injunction

As much as the AHM's argues that the FDA based their approval of the chemical abortion drug on politics, the defendants claim the plaintiffs' arguments are speculative at best, as well as untimely, unexhausted, and without merit (Godfrey and Papagiannopoulos, 2024).

In their complaint, the government argues that the FDA is responsible to ensure that new drugs it authorizes are safe and effective for their intended use and rebuts allegations by the AHM that their approval of the chemical abortion drug fell below or outside necessary standards (Alliance for Hippocratic Medicine, et al., v U.S. Food and Drug Administration, et al., 2022). The FDA derives part of this authority from the Federal Food, Drug, and Cosmetic Act, which prohibits the interstate distribution of new drugs that have not gone through formal FDA approval. The FDA argues that all their approvals are based on scientific evidence that the drug being considered is safe and effective for its intended purposes. The FDA argues that whenever a drug's sponsors submit a supplemental new drug application these same standards apply. Furthermore, when a generic version is being considered, the FDA states that their review ensures it is materially the same as the approved drug *Food and Drug Administration, 2023*

The FDA explains that in the original approval process from 1996 to 2000 of the chemical abortion drug, that they determined through multiple studies, that all evidence showed the use of the drug was safe and effective for its intended purposes and its distribution outweighed any risks. The FDA also affirmed that in using Subpart H, they were able to place restrictions on in-person dispensing requirements and agreed prescriptions for the drug would be given by or under the supervision of a physician that could accurately date pregnancy and diagnosis ectopic pregnancies. This is why in 2002, when the plaintiffs, the AAPLOG and the Christian Medical Association (CMA) submitted a citizens petition (which is required before asking a court to invalidate the FDA's authorization of a drug), the FDA rejected it on March 29, 2016 (*Alliance for Hippocratic Medicine, et al., v. Us. Food and Drug Administration, et al. Defendant's Opposition to Plaintiff's Motion for a Preliminary Injunction, 2023, pp.1–6*)

However, in 2016, in relying on more studies on the chemical abortion drug, the FDA increased the gestational age limit from forty-nine to seventy days, reduced the numbers of visits from one to three, and recognized at home distribution as safe because research showed mifepristone was associated with an "exceedingly low rates of serious adverse events," and that there was no significant difference among patients who followed up on the phone with their healthcare provider when being distributed the drug versus those who did so in person (*Alliance for Hippocratic Medicine, et al., v. Us. Food and Drug Administration, et al. Defendant's Opposition to Plaintiff's Motion for a Preliminary Injunction, 2023,*p. 5). However, during this time, the FDA also expanded the healthcare providers who could distribute the drug outside of physicians if they were also certified under the agency's Risk Evaluation and Mitigation Strategy (REMS) process, which is required for certain medications with any serious safety concerns to ensure the benefits of the therapeutic outweigh risks. Furthermore, the FDA explains that in 2019, when the agency approved the generic version of the chemical abortion drug it was deemed to be materially same as the originally approved drug, so there was nothing that the organization did to breach protocol (*Alliance for Hippocratic Medicine, et al., v. Us. Food and Drug Administration, et al. Defendants' Opposition to the Plaintiffs' Motion for* a *Preliminary Injunction,* 2023, pp. 5–6).

In 2019, the plaintiffs, AAPLOG, and the American College of Pediatricians (ACP) submitted a second citizen petition, challenging the 2016 changes to the conditions of the approval, including REMS; however, this petition did not ask the agency to withdraw approval of mifepristone. Instead, the petition requested the FDA to retain the REMS and in-person dispensing of the drug and return to the approval requirements of 2000, such as limiting mifepristone's use to a forty-nine day gestation period, requiring the medication to only be given by or under the supervision of a physically present, certified physician, require the original three office visits, supply a contraindication for patients without regular access to emergency medical care, mandate reporting of adverse effects, and continue additional studies on the regimen (*Alliance for Hippocratic Medicine, et al., v. Us. Food and Drug Administration, et al. Defendant's Opposition to Plaintiff's Motion for a Preliminary Injunction, 2023,*pp. 6–7). However, the FDA continued to relax restrictions on the drug in April 2021 during the COVID-19 pandemic by permitting it to be mailed and took note of a six-month evaluation period where no evidence of serious safety concerns developed. On January 3, 2023, the FDA removed the in-person dispensing requirement completely (*Alliance for Hippocratic Medicine, et al., v. Us. Food and Drug Administration, et al. Defendant's Opposition to Plaintiff's Motion for a Preliminary Injunction, 2023, p.* 6).

In the original complaint, the FDA argues that the plaintiffs have shown little likelihood of success on the merits and their claims are speculative. The FDA also argues the plaintiff does not show injury, which is a key element to stand before a court and present a case, and that, therefore, they are outside of the proper zone of interests and are not cognizable under Article III. However, the FDA does concede that the only possible issue with merit that the plaintiffs have in their complaint to be heard by the Court are those in their 2019 citizen petition (*Alliance for Hippocratic Medicine, et al., v. Us. Food and Drug Administration, et al. Defendant's Opposition to Plaintiff's Motion for a Preliminary Injunction, 2023*, pp .1, 9). Other than this issue, opposition holds that the plaintiff's arguments are likely to fail on their merits, the studies they present do not undermine the authority of the FDA, and their request for a preliminary injunction would not only harm the public interests by withdrawing a safe and effective drug, but comprise state healthcare systems, disrupt businesses in the sale and distribution of mifepristone, and interfere with Congress' ability to entrust the FDA to guarantee the safety and efficacy of approving drugs (*Alliance for Hippocratic Medicine, et al., v. Us. Food and Drug Administration, et al. Defendant's Opposition to Plaintiff's Motion for a Preliminary Injunction, 2023,*pp. 20–22, 34–40).

Judge Kacsmaryk District Court Order and Opinion

On April 7, 2023, Judge Matthew Kacsmaryk granted the plaintiff's (the Alliance for Hippocratic Medicine et al.) motion in part by staying the FDA's approval of mifepristone. Judge Kacsmaryk stayed the applicability of the order for seven days to permit the federal government time to seek immediate relief from the US Court of Appeals for the Fifth Circuit (*Alliance for Hippocratic Medicine et al v. U.S. Food and Drug Administration et al.*, 2023, p. 67).

In his opinion, Judge Kacsmaryk addressed several key issues. Kacsmaryk immediately accused the FDA of ignoring the plaintiff's 2002 citizens petition where they requested the agency to stay the approval of Mifeprex (mifepristone) and halt all distribution and marketing of the drug pending the final action on the petition because the FDA had used the Subpart H process to expedite the drug's approval by categorizing it as treatment for a serious or life-threatening illness (*Alliance for Hippocratic Medicine et al v. U.S. Food and Drug Administration et al.,* 2023,1–2). Judge Kacsmaryk added that in 2006, the House of Representatives' Subcommittee on Criminal Justice, Drug Policy, and Human Resources expressed similar concerns and investigated the FDA's handling of mifepristone, finding it was associated with "the death of eight women, nine life-threatening incidents, two hundred and thirty-two hospitalization, a hundred sixteen blood transfusions, and eighty-eight cases of infection" (*Alliance for Hippocratic Medicine et al v. U.S. Food and Drug Administration et al.,* 2023,p. 4).

Kacsmaryk also attacked arguments made by the FDA against the AHM in their response to the plaintiff's complaint. For instance, Kacsmaryk argued that the plaintiffs can stand before the court because they have associational standing due to the AHM's members ability to claim adverse events can occur because of chemical abortion drugs overwhelming the medical system and putting "enormous pressure and stress" on physician during emergencies, which can consume crucial and scarce resources, particularly in areas where there is limited doctor availability (*Alliance for Hippocratic Medicine et al v. U.S. Food and* Drug Administration et al., 2023,p. 7). Kacsmaryk also agreed with the plaintiffs that the medical associations that are party to their claim have standing since they are "opposed to being forced to end the life of a human being in the womb for no medical reason, including by having to complete an incomplete elective chemical abortion" (*Alliance for Hippocratic Medicine et al v. U.S. Food and Drug Administration et al.*, 2023, p. 8). Furthermore, Kacsmaryk said that the plaintiffs have organizational standing by showing the defendant's actions drain their organizations' resources and cause them adverse effects. He further held that the affiliated medical associations to the plaintiff's claim also have organizational standing due to the FDA's failure to require the reporting of adverse events from those taking the abortion pill and that this comprises these groups ability to educate and inform their member physicians, patients, and the public of the dangers the drug poses (*Alliance for Hippocratic Medicine et al v. U.S. Food and Drug Administration et al.,* 2023,11–12).

Furthermore, Kacsmaryk held that the FDA's 2016 and 2021 changes significantly departed from the original approved drug scheme. And, that the agency's review of the plaintiff's 2019 petition, which was completed in 2021, essentially reaffirmed their substantive reconsideration of the abortion pill and its potential dangers. Therefore, Kacsmaryk held any statute of limitations period for the plaintiffs to contest the FDA's authorization of the abortion pill begins in 2021 and the AHM is not time barred in bringing the case to the court under the principle of equitable tolling, which gives the court discretion to extend a deadline due to extraordinary circumstances that inhibited an individual's timely action (Cornell Legal Information Institute, 2023; *United States v. Patterson* (5th Cir. 2000)). Kacsmaryk argued that because of the FDA's "unreasonable delay" in responding to both the plaintiffs 2002 and 2019 petitions, equitable tolling was appropriate in terms of the AHM ability to stand before the court on their claim (*Alliance for Hippocratic Medicine et al v. U.S. Food and Drug Administration et al.,* 2023, p. 24).

Regarding the FDA's 2021 changes removing the in-person dispensing requirement of the chemical abortion pill, Kacsmaryk argued that the agency did not have the authority for such action. Kacsmaryk held that under Heckler v. Chaney (1985), the FDA may have discretion in "one-off" decisions, but it does not have the authority to "suspend entire statutes" and therefore, any exception to judicial review is very narrow (*Alliance for Hippocratic Medicine et al v. U.S. Food and* Drug Administration et al., 2023,p. 26). Additionally, the AHM argued that the FDA's 2021 decision to dispense mifepristone via mail did not address federal criminal laws prohibiting such distribution. The FDA countered that the AHM did not exhaust its arguments on this issue because it did not present the matter at any stage of the administrative proceedings on the dispensing of the drug via mail. Kacsmaryk held that the AHM's failure to exhaust claims through the administrative process did not preclude judicial review because exhaustion is not required where an agency is found to act in excess of its authority. Therefore, a court will review "a particular challenge to an agency's decision which was not raised during the agency proceedings" (*Myron v. Martin* (5th Cir. 1982); *Alliance for Hippocratic Medicine et al v. U.S. Food and Drug Administration et al.,* 2023, p. 27).

In his opinion, Kacsmaryk went on to address several other issues in favor of the plaintiffs, such as public policy concerns surrounding the applicability of the Comstock Act, originally enacted in 1873 and which currently includes section 1462, prohibiting the mailing of obscene or crime-inciting matter, including "every article or thing designed, adapted, or intended for producing abortion…" (18 USC 1461). Kacsmaryk held that, along with the concerns over individual injury and injustice that may result from the use of mifepristone, the FDA's administrative procedures were inadequate, as evidenced by their slow response time to the plaintiffs' petitions and the suspension of the requirement of abortion practitioners to report non-fatal adverse events. He further stated that the plaintiffs will be successful on the merits due to the FDA violating federal law on mail dispensing, categorizing pregnancy as an illness and thus violating Subpart H for the Accelerated Approval of New Drugs for Serious or Life-Threatening Illness (*Alliance for Hippocratic Medicine et al v. U.S. Food and Drug Administration et al.,* 2023, pp. 29–50).

The Aftermath of the District Court Ruling

Within a week of the District Court's decision, the FDA applied for a stay of Judge Kacsmaryk's ruling. However, on April 12, 2023, the US Court of Appeals for the Fifth Circuit issued a ruling refusing to block Judge Kacsmaryk's decision at the District Court and attempted to reinstate pre-2016 restrictions on the chemical abortion pill. As a result, on April 14, 2023, the FDA filed an application for emergency relief from the US Supreme Court (Center for Reproductive Rights, 2024). By this time, Danco Laboratories, LLC, a pharmaceutical corporation that solely distributes Mifeprex, intervened in the case on side of the FDA Center for Reproductive Rights, 2024. On April 21, 2023, the FDA's application for a stay was granted by the Supreme Court, "pending disposition of the appeal in the US Court of Appeals for the Fifth Circuit and disposition of a petition for writ of certiorari, if such a writ is timely sought" (*Danco Laboratories, LLC v. Alliance for Hippocratic Medicine, et al. On Application for Stay*, 2023, p.1).2023

The case was then filed before the Fifth Circuit. On August 16, 2023, after officially hearing the appeal, the court vacated in part and affirmed in part the District Court's stay order. Specifically, the appellate court held that the medical organizations and doctors' concerns regarding the accelerated approval process of mifepristone were likely barred by the statute of limitations, keeping the drug available to public under 2016 conditions. The Fifth Circuit also vacated the part of the district court's order on the 2019 generic approval because the medical organizations and doctors who were party to the claim did not show how the generic version of mifepristone caused them injury. However, the court of appeal affirmed the portions of the stay order concerning the 2016 Amendments to the drug protocol (i.e., the change in dosage, decreased number of required visits for medical consultation, exceptions to who could prescribe the drug, and the removal of reporting non-fatal complications from the medications use) affirmed, along with the district court's ruling on the 2021 Non-Enforcement Decision permitting mifepristone to be distributed by mail (*Alliance for Hippocratic Medicine et al. v. U.S. Food & Drug Administration et al. and Danco Laboratories, LLC.* (5th Cir. 2023)). However, the Supreme Court of the United States issued a stay on April 21, 2023, pending a final disposition on appeal, which superseded this decision.

Also following the Fifth Circuit's ruling, on September 8, 2023, both the FDA and Danco Laboratories, LLC filed a petition for writ of certiorari to the US Supreme Court to formally hear their case against the AHM. On December 13, 2023, the Supreme Court announced the cases were consolidated and the petitions for certiorari were granted, meaning the Court would officially hear and rule on the case during its 2023–2024 calendar (SCOTUSblog.com, 2023).

On March 26, 2024, the Supreme Court of the United States heard arguments in *U.S. Food & Drug Administration v. Alliance for Hippocratic*. The main issues evaluated before the Supreme Court during oral arguments centered on: (1) whether the respondents, Alliance for Hippocratic Medicine et al., have Article III standing to challenge the FDA's 2016 and 2021 actions easing access to mifepristone; (2) if the FDA's actions in 2016 and 2021 were arbitrary and capricious; and (3) if the lower district court properly granted preliminary relief. During oral arguments, the government claimed that millions of Americans have safely used mifepristone, the Alliance does not have proper standing and, therefore, cannot rely on the theory of injury pronounced by the District Court. The government also argued that the AHM's position relies on too many "remote contingencies," as only an exceptionally small number of women have experienced serious side effects from the drug, and their arguments on harmfulness are "speculative" *Food and Drug Administration, et al., v Alliance for Hippocratic Medicine, et al*, Oral Argument Transcript, 2024p. 5). The government also argued that the FDA decision to ease access to mifepristone was based on dozens of studies and that granting the respondents relief would cause major disruption to the federal system of both developing and approving drugs, causing harm to not only the FDA but the pharmaceutical industry. Furthermore, the government argued that the agency conducts routine surveillance of drugs, adjusting regulatory schemes if safety concerns emerge, and that the liability for harm to patients always rests with drug sponsors. When challenged by the justices on the respondent's arguments that mifepristone by mail saw an increase in emergency room visits by patients, the government rebutted that these trips did not equate to serious adverse events for women. Danco Laboratories, manufacturers of mifepristone, also argued that the changes in access to the drug resulted in more reporting to the FDA on adverse reactions.

The respondents, the AHM, countered the FDA in oral arguments by claiming that the FDA's approval of mifepristone by mail was based on inadequate data, so the district court's decision simply restored critical protections to women using the drug. The AHM also argued that by not giving the Alliance standing, health care practitioners would be forced to violate their consciences by being put in a position to manage abortions in the event of a woman's adverse reaction to mifepristone, causing the doctor professional harm without judicial recourse. Essentially, the AHM argued that doctors and healthcare professionals they represent should receive a form of third-party standing, which allows another person or entity to assert the rights of individuals when their interests are closely aligned, and it is difficult for that person to assert their own rights. What is interesting is that third-party standing has usually been invoked by doctors in abortion cases challenging the constitutionality of restrictions on the procedure. However, here, the AHM attempted to use the principle to argue that to prevent standing denies these healthcare practitioners individual recourse or rights (*Food and Drug Administration, et al., v Alliance for Hippocratic Medicine, et al*, Oral Argument Transcript, 2024, pp. 62–63, 66, 74–111).). Again, this approach is aligned with Lewis' (2017) claims that conservatives are beginning to use an individual rights-based approach when fighting progressive abortion policies, to secure their rights to things like conscience protection, religious liberty, and access to the courts.

During oral arguments, the justices seemed to be concerned whether the AHM and the doctors they represented had proper standing to bring a lawsuit against the FDA. The Supreme Court also appeared to have concerns about whether the lower courts' decisions on the case went too far in scrutinizing the FDA and if the courts have the proper knowledge to make determinations on the agency's regulation of drugs, such as mifepristone. (Suhasini and Reingold, 2024). On June 13, 2024, the Supreme Court issued its official decision in the case, ruling in favor of the FDA. The Supreme Court came to its decision by holding that the AHM did not have proper standing to sue the FDA because the lack the ability to demonstrate that injury was done to the doctors and medical organizations the AHM represented (*Food and Drug Administration et al. v. Alliance for Hippocratic Medicine et al.* (2024). This case will be further discussed in Chapter 4.

Lobbying over Chemical Abortion

In evaluating how access to the abortion pill is now at the Supreme Court, it is important to understand some of the first ideas behind the population control movement in the United States, as well as efforts to bring RU 486 to the market, and how the COVID-19 pandemic ushered in an era of lobbying on the topic of self-managed abortion. These underlying dynamics provide additional context for where and why the United States is on access to mifepristone.

As previously mentioned, Roussel Uclaf, the French manufacturer of the chemical abortion pill, RU-486, was lobbied by the Clinton Administration to give their patent rights to the nonprofit group, the Population Council, so the medication could be distributed in the United States. The Population Council would eventually grant Danco Laborites an "exclusive license to manufacture and distribute Mifeprex in the United States" (*Alliance for Hippocratic Medicine et al. v. U.S. Food & Drug Administration et al. and Danco Laboratories, LLC.* (5th Cir. 2023), 5). So, who is the Population Council, and why were they selected as the organization to contract with Roussel Uclaf? Well, the Population Council was first founded through the Rockefeller Brothers Fund in 1952 with an interest in global population growth, family planning, and the health and development of nations. Trustee, John D. Rockefeller III, began to work on population control efforts from the standpoint of human fertility and contraception research, which included access to affordable birth control. The Council funded research on increasing access to contraception among racial minorities and the poor, while some members also focused on controlling the population growth among white and economically well-off families (The Population Council, 2023; Ziegler, 2013).

The population control movement, which the Council played an influential role in, began to develop after World War II as concerns with overpopulation gained traction and the US government engaged in family planning policy under the Social Security Act, opened foreign aid on the issue to developing countries. And, under President Nixon, the National Center for Population and Family Planning was created within the Department of Health, Education, and Welfare. The Population Movement was both influential and diverse, as evidenced by Nixon receiving bipartisan support for the Family Planning Services and Population Research Act of 1970 (Ziegler, 2013). As the Population Movement continued to grow, there was a split among some who did and did not support legalizing abortion. Members who endorsed the legalization of abortion were linked to issues such as the sexual revolution, women's movement, and environmental stewardship. However, there was no formal position among the Population Council endorsing legal abortion pre-*Roe* (Ziegler, 2013). Yet, once *Roe v. Wade* (1973) appeared before the Supreme Court, concerns over population control began to change and the focus turned to issues of privacy and their relation to procreation, marriage, and contraception in deciding that women had a constitutional right to terminate their pregnancies up to the point of viability (Ziegler, 2013; *Roe v. Wade,* 1973).

In the aftermath of *Roe*, the pro-Choice movement stepped away from arguments surrounding population in advocating for abortion. Arguments among pro-choice circles began focusing more women's bodily autonomy, societal equality, and increased access to reproductive rights and healthcare (Ziegler, 2013). In the 1980s, US feminist groups, such as the Feminist Majority Foundation (FMF), Reproductive Health and Technology Project (RHTP), Abortion Rights Mobilization (ARM), Planned Parenthood (PP), and the National Abortion and Reproductive Rights Action League (NARAL) had been paying attention to the development of RU-486 in France and urged the French manufacturer to bring it to US markets (Jackman, 2002). However, Roussel Uclaf was hesitant to bring mifepristone to the United States due to fear of anti-abortion boycotts, hostility toward the medication by the Bush Administration, and concerns about anti-abortion violence (Jackman, 2002; Dorozynski, 1997). At first the pressure from anti-abortion activist, such as the National Right to Life Committee, Catholic hospitals, and conservative members of Congress were successful in getting the FDA's then-Commissioner, Frank Young in 1989 to issue a ban on RU-486 being brought into the United States (Jackman, 2002). Jackman (2002) argues this marked the point when the strategy to bring mifepristone to the United States shifted from solely a traditional governmental lobbying standpoint to one that also included a strategy of independent campaigns among feminist social groups. Some of these efforts included the FMF launching a national education initiative on mifepristone. The FMF also led a delegation of medical practitioners and researchers that met with officials of Roussel Uclaf, signaling the American scientific community's support of the drug. From this point, the FMF engaged state legislatures to pass resolutions in support of making RU-486 available in the United States. Other groups, such as the RHTP worked with NARAL, Population Crisis Committee, the Population Council, and the National Women's Health Network to survey politicians on their positions, develop media campaigns, and promote research on the mifepristone. For example, between October of 1989 and April 1994, the FMF and their network mailed eight million letters and petitions to women's rights supporters containing educational information about mifepristone. These materials were sent to both Hoechst AG (former German parent company of Roussel Uclaf) and Roussel Uclaf to show these companies that public support for mifepristone was surpassing the opposition in the United States.

As part of a multi-pronged approach to bring attention to and overturn the FDA's import ban on mifepristone, ARM challenged the policy by having a pregnant woman, Leona Benten, bring the drug through US customs on a flight from London to New York's John F. Kennedy International Airport. As part of the plan, Lawrence Lader, an abortion rights leader, organized the trip and notified authorities in advance of what Benten was doing (Bella, 2023; ,). A legal battle ensued, with the District Court granting a preliminary injunction compelling the drug to be returned to Benten. The Court of Appeals stayed the District Court's decision, pending an appeal. Finally, the Supreme Court of the United States in a seven to two decision denied the application to vacate the stay, stating that the applicant (Benten) did not demonstrate a substantial likelihood of her claim on the merits and the drug was not approved by the FDA. Jackman (2002) argues that though this case was not successful in terms of lifting the FDA's ban, it succeeded in garnering wide media coverage and by the time Roussel Uclaf announced it was donating its patent rights to the nonprofit, Population Council in 1994, most all the country's major newspapers published editorials supporting the drug's availability in the United States. Overtime, feminist organizations turned the anti-abortion threats of violence on their head by pushing RU-486 to be made available in the United States through doctors' offices because it would cut down on pro-life extremists protesting outside of clinics. This argument was also picked up by media outlets.

Yet, one of the biggest challenges of getting RU-486 accessible to US markets was the Bush Administration. Again, to work around the Bush Administration, the FMF launched a national campaign to get state and local municipalities, as well as Congress, to pass resolutions supporting the accessibility of RU-486. States such as New Hampshire, California, Hawaii, and Maine participated in this effort, as well as New York City. Members of Congress, such as Representatives Ron Wyden (Democrat or Oregon), Patricia Schroeder (Democrat of Colorado), and

Senator Paul Wellstone (Democrat of Minnesota), called for hearings on the drug and sponsored legislation to remove the FDA's import alert on the medication and call for clinic testing (Jackman, 2002).

Finally, the election of President Bill Clinton in 1992 provided the final round of pressure on Roussel Uclaf to apply to the FDA for the approval of RU-486 (Thoss, 1993). And, within the first days of Clinton's inauguration, the President issued an executive order revoking the prohibitions on the importation of RU-486 (Tumulty and Cimons, 1993). By 1994, Roussel Uclaf had agreed to donate its patent on the drug to the Population Council. By 2000, the medicated abortion became available under the FDA's approval in the United States (Saul, 1999).

References

Alliance for Hippocratic Medicine, et al., v. Us. Food and Drug Administration, et al. Defendant's Opposition to Plaintiff's Motion for a Preliminary Injunction (2023). Available at: https://www.justice.gov/reproductive-rights/media/1269071/dl?inline= (Accessed 5 June 2023).

Alliance for Hippocratic Medicine v. U.S. Food and Drug Administration (2022) United States District Court for the Northern District of Texas Amarillo Division, *Case* 2:22-cv-0223-Z. Available at: https://adflegal-live-drupal-files-delivery.s3.amazonaws.com/public/2022-11/Alliance-for-Hippocratic-Medicine-v-FDA-2022-11-18-Complaint.pdf (Accessed: 5 June 2023).

Alliance for Hippocratic Medicine (2023a) *Upholding and Promoting the Fundamental Principles of Hippocratic Medicine.* Available at: https://allianceforhippocraticmedicine.org (Accessed: 5 June 2023).

Alliance for Hippocratic Medicine (2023b) *Supreme Court Weighs Restoring Safety Standards for Abortion Drugs.* Available at: https://adflegal.org/article/supreme-court-weighs-restoring-safety-standards-abortion-drugs#:~:text=Case%20timeline&text=September%202000%3A%20The%20FDA%20approved,FDA%20denied%20the%20citizen%20petition (Accessed: 5 June 2023).

Bella, T. (2023) 'The Abortion Pill's 1992 Supreme Court Battle and the Woman Who Started It', *The Washington Post*, 8 April. Available at: https://www.washingtonpost.com/politics/2023/04/08/abortion-pill-mifepristone-leona-benten/ (Accessed: 7 May 2024).

Center for Reproductive Rights (2024) *Alliance for Hippocratic Medicine v. FDA.* Available at: https://reproductiverights.org/case/alliance-for-hippocratic-medicine-v-fda/ (Accessed 19 June 2025).

Chemerinsky, E. (2023) 'Why One Judge in Amarillo Got to Decide Whether any American Could Use the Abortion Pill', *Los Angeles Times*. vailable at: https://www.latimes.com/opinion/story/2023-04-25/supreme-court-mifepristone-ruling-abortion-judges (Accessed: 2 October 2023).

Cillizza, C. (2022) 'The Bottom is Dropping out of the 2022 Election for Democrats', *CNN*. Available at: https://www.cnn.com/2022/11/01/politics/democratic-seats-jeopardy-gallup-polling (Accessed: 2 October 2023).

Cornell Law School Legal Information Institute (2023) *Erie Doctrine*. Available at: https://www.law.cornell.edu/wex/erie_doctrine#:~:text=The%20Erie%20doctrine%20is%20a,Court%20case%2C%20Erie%20Railroad%20Co (Accessed: 2 October 2023).

Danco Laboratories, LLC v. Alliance for Hippocratic Medicine, et al. On Application for Stay (2023). United States Supreme Court. Available at: https://reproductiverights.org/wp-content/uploads/2023/04/Supreme-court-order-stay-FDA-4-21-23.pdf (Accessed: 5 June 2023).

Dorozynski, A. (1997) 'Boycott Threats Forces French Company to Abandon RU486', *British Medical Journal*, 314(7088), p.1150. Available at: doi: https://doi.org/10.1136/bmj.314.7088.1145m (Accessed: 7 May 2024).

First Liberty Institute (2023) First Liberty: *Your First Call*. Available at: https://firstliberty.org/about-us/ (Accessed: 2 October 2023).

Food and Drug Administration et al. *v. Alliance for Hippocratic Medicine* et al. *and Danco Laboratories, L.L.C. v. Alliance for Hippocratic Medicine et al.* (2024a) United States Supreme Court, case 23-235 and 23-236. Available at: https://www.supremecourt.gov/oral_arguments/argument_transcripts/2023/23-235_p8k0.pdf (Accessed: 17 April 2024).

Food and Drug Administration, et al., v Alliance for Hippocratic Medicine, et al, Oral Argument Transcript, (2024). United States Supreme Court and Heritage Reporting Corporation. Available at: https://www.supremecourt.gov/oral_arguments/audio/2023/23-235 (Accessed 19 June 2025).

Food and Drug Administration et al. v. Alliance for Hippocratic Medicine et al. (2024) United States Supreme Court. Available at: https://www.supremecourt.gov/opinions/23pdf/23-235_n7ip.pdf (Accessed: 13 June 2024).

Food and Drug Administration (2023) *Information about Mifepristone for Medical Termination of Pregnancy Through Ten Weeks Gestation*. Available at https://www.fda.gov/drugs/postmarket-drug-safety-information-patients-and-providers/information-about-mifepristone-medical-termination-pregnancy-through-ten-weeks-gestation#:~:text=Mifeprex%20(mifepristone)%20and%20its%20generic,a%20patient%27s%20last%20menstrual%20period) (Accessed: 2 October 2023).

Godfrey, B. and Papagiannopoulos, T (2024) 'Alliance for Hippocratic Medicine v. U.S. Food and Drug Administration', *Food & Drug Law Institute*, 22 May. Available at: https://www.fdli.org/2024/05/alliance-for-hippocratic-medicine-v-u-s-food-and-drug-administration/#:~:text=The%20defendants'%20opposition%20to%20the%20plaintiffs'%20motion%20for%20preliminary%20injunction,statute%20of%20limitations;%203)%20the (Accessed 18 June 2025).

Harvard Library (2001). The Story of RU-468 in the United States. Available at: https://dash.harvard.edu/server/api/core/bitstreams/7312037c-ad68-6bd4-e053-0100007fdf3b/content (Accessed 19 June 2025).

Hammonds, C. (2023) '10 Things to Know About Alliance for Hippocratic Medicine v. FDA', *Progressive Caucus Center*, 25 April. Available at: https://www.progressivecaucuscenter.org/alliance-for-hippocratic-medicine-v-fda#:~:text=The%20Alliance%20for%20Hippocratic%20Medicine%20(AHM)%20is%20a%20Tennessee%2D,months%20after%20the%20Dobbs%20decision (Accessed: 5 June 2023).

Hartig, H. (2022) 'About Six-in-Ten Americans Say Abortion Should Be Legal in All or Most Cases', *Pew Research Center*, 13 June. Available at: https://www.pewresearch.org/short-reads/2022/06/13/about-six-in-ten-americans-say-abortion-should-be-legal-in-all-or-most-cases-2/ (Accessed: 2 October 2023).

Heckler v. Chaney, 470 U.S. 821 (1985)

Jackman, J. (2002) 'Anatomy of a Feminist Victory: Wining the Transfer of RU 486 Patent Rights to the United States, 1988–1994', *Women & Politics*, 24(3), pp.81–99. Available at: https://doi.org/10.1300/J014v24n03_05 (Accessed: 7 May 2024).

Kurtzleben, D. (2022) 'What we Know (and don't know) About How Abortion Affected the Midterms', *NPR*. Available at: https://www.npr.org/2022/11/25/1139040227/abortion-midterm-elections-2022-republicans-democrats-roe-dobbs (Accessed: 2 October 2023).

Lampe, J.R. (2022) 'Where a Suit Can Proceed: Court Selection and Forum Shopping', *Congressional Research Service*. pp. 1–5. Available at: https://crsreports.congress.gov/product/pdf/LSB/LSB10856 (Accessed: 2 October 2023).

Lewis, A. (2017) *The Rights Turn in Conservative Christian Politics: How Abortion Transformed the Culture Wars*. United Kingdom: Cambridge University Press.

Mayo Clinic (2023) *Mifepristone (Oral Route)*. Available at: https://www.mayoclinic.org/drugs-supplements/mifepristone-oral-route/side-effects/drg-20067123?p=1#:~:text=Mifepristone%20is%20used%20in%20a,of%20the%20uterus%20are%20expelled (Accessed: 2 October 2023).

Monyak, S., and Wheeler, L. (2024) 'Republicans Suggest Judges Can Ignore Forum-Shopping Curb (2)', *Bloomberg Law*, 14 March. Available at https://news.bloomberglaw.com/us-law-week/judge-shopping-curb-draws-partisan-backlash-in-senate (Accessed: 10 April 2024).

National Association for the Repeal of Abortion Laws. *Alliance for Hippocratic Medicine v. FDA Court Case*. Available at: https://reproductivefreedomforall.

org/news/alliance-for-hippocratic-medicine-v-fda-court-case/ (Accessed: 2 October 2023).

National Library of Medicine. (2024). *Mifepristone*. Available at: https://www.ncbi.nlm.nih.gov/books/NBK557612/ (Accessed: 10 April 2024).

NBC News (2016) *Trump: 'I Will Be Appointing Pro-Life Judges.'* Available at: https://www.nbcnews.com/video/trump-i-will-be-appointing-pro-life-judges-789632067780 (Accessed: 2 October 2023).

Paris, D., and Cohn, N. (2022) 'After Roe's End, Women Surged in Signing Up to Vote in Some States', *The New York Times*, 25 August. Available at: https://www.nytimes.com/interactive/2022/08/25/upshot/female-voters-dobbs.html (Accessed: 2 October 2023).

Reingold, R. (2020) 'Standing in June Medical Services v. Russo Explained', *O'Neill Institute for national and Global Health Law, Georgetown Law*. Available at: https://oneill.law.georgetown.edu/standing-in-june-medical-services-v-russo-explained/ (Accessed: 17 April 2024).

Roe v. Wade, 410 U.S. 113 (1973)

Saul, R. (1999) 'The Political Challenges and Educational Opportunities Very Early Abortion', *Guttmacher Institute*, 1 February. Available at: https://www.guttmacher.org/gpr/1999/02/political-challenges-and-educational-opportunities-very-early-abortion (Accessed: 7 May 2024).

Schneider, E., and Otterein, H. (2022) 'The Central Issue': How the Fall of Roe v. Wade Shook the 2022 Election', *Politico*. Available at: https://www.politico.com/news/2022/12/19/dobbs-2022-election-abortion-00074426 (Accessed: 2 October 2023).

Scotusblog (2023) *Food and Drug Administration v. Alliance for Hippocratic Medicine*. Available at: https://www.scotusblog.com/cases/case-files/food-and-drug-administration-v-alliance-for-hippocratic-medicine-2/ (Accessed 19 June 2025).

Suhasini, R., and Reingold, R. (2024) 'FDA v. Alliance for Hippocratic Medicine: Recapping the Supreme Court's Oral Arguments', *O'Neill Institute for national and Global Health Law, Georgetown Law*. Available at: https://oneill.law.georgetown.edu/fda-v-alliance-for-hippocratic-medicine-recapping-the-supreme-courts-oral-argument/ (Accessed: 17 April 2024).

The Federalist Society (2023) *Hon. Matthey J. Kacsmaryk*. Available at: https://fedsoc.org/contributors/matthew-kacsmaryk (Accessed: 2 October 2023).

The Population Council (2023) *About*. Available at: https://www.rbf.org/about/our-history/timeline/population-council (Accessed 5 June 2023).

Thoss, E. (1993) 'Introduction of RU 486 in the USA: Obstacles and Opportunities', *Plan Parent Europe Journal*, 22(3), pp.18–9. Available at: https://pubmed.ncbi.nlm.nih.gov/12288950/ (Accessed: 7 May 2024).

Tumulty, K., and Cimons, M. (1993) 'Clinton Revokes Abortion Curbs: Executive Orders: President Ends Ban on Fetal Tissue Research, Overturns Gag Rule at Clinics and Clears Way for the FDA to Allow Importing of French RU 486 Pill', *Los Angeles Times*, 23 January. Available at: https://www.

latimes.com/archives/la-xpm-1993-01-23-mn-1587-story.html (Accessed: 7 May 2024).

United States Code Chapter 18 Section 1461. *Library of Congress*. Available at: https://tile.loc.gov/storage-services/service/ll/uscode/uscode1946-00801/uscode1946-008018071/uscode1946-008018071.pdf?loclr=bloglaw (Accessed: 15 June 2024).

Wheeler, L. (2023a) 'Two Judges, Two Abortion Pill Rulings-'Totally Different Worlds', *Bloomberg Law*, 10 April. Available at: https://news.bloomberglaw.com/us-law-week/two-judges-two-abortion-pill-rulings-totally-different-worlds (Accessed: 5 June 2023).

Wheeler, R. (2024). 'Effort to Curb Judge-Shopping at the Federal Courts Explained', *Brookings*, 18 April. Available at: https://www.brookings.edu/articles/effort-to-curb-judge-shopping-at-the-federal-courts-explained/ (Accessed 25 April 2024).

Ziegler, M. (2013) 'Roe's Race: The Supreme Court, Population Control, and Reproductive Justice', *Yale Journal of Law & Feminism*, 25(1), pp.1–50. Available at: https://ir.law.fsu.edu/articles/327/ (Accessed: 7 May 2024).

3

RED STATES V. BLUE STATES AND THE REGULATION OF REPRODUCTIVE RIGHTS IN A POST-*DOBBS* AMERICA

Though Supreme Court rulings, such as *Roe v. Wade* (1973) and *Planned Parenthood v.* Casey (1992), maintained that women had a constitutional right to an abortion, they recognized states' interest in regulating access to the procedure. However, in a post-*Dobbs* America, where there is no constitutional guarantee barring states from prohibiting access to abortion, the country is left with a checkered map, with some states having wide-ranging access to reproductive healthcare, while others have limited to no options at all for women looking to terminate their pregnancies. The differences in level of access to abortion across the country tend to vary on the political make-up of each state, with liberal or Democratic states having more protective measures to secure women's access to abortion services and conservative states being more restrictive (Guttmacher Institute, 2024).

Table 3.1 below shows the states with the most restrictive versus more protective access to abortion services in the country. The table shows that states that restrict abortion access tend to be run by the Republican Party in terms of who controls the governorship and state legislature, while more progressive states that permit abortion are led by the Democratic Party. On average, restrictive states are made up of more people who identify as Christian (78.2% and from this, 37.6% who are evangelical Protestant) compared to progressive states, which on average are 65% Christian, with an evangelical Protestant population averaging 17.12% (Pew Research Center, 2024). It is important to evaluate how religious affiliation influences abortion policies because religion is a complex and multifaceted construct that can inform

DOI: 10.4324/9781032636177-3

political attitudes and processes (Wald et al., 1988). However, some political and religious scholars argue that to better understand the role religion may play in the legislative process, it is important to consider not only affiliation but saliency and advocacy. With regards to saliency, scholars should pay closer attention to religiosity, such as the level of devotionalism and participation in services, as well as how orthodox some policy makers may be in terms of their religious beliefs or their subscription to biblical literalism, which appear to be important when understanding the role religion may play in legislative behavior (Yamane and Oldmixon, 2006).

In their work on roll call voting in state legislators, Yamane and Oldmixon (2006) find that political and demographic factors dominate direct effects on abortion policy. However, Oldmixon and Yamane note in terms of demographic variables, religion did not have a significant, direct effect on abortion voting policy, though conservative Protestants were more positively associated with pro-life voting positions. Oldmixon and Yamane suggest that religious saliency influences a worldview that impacts a range of attitudes and positions across legislators, not just morality political issues like abortion. Furthermore, Oldmixon and Yamane's findings seem to challenge the notion that abortion politics are primarily tied up with religious politics and are polarized along party lines.

And, in their work on targeted regulation of abortion providers (TRAP), Medoff and Dennis (2011) argue that these policies impose medically unnecessary and unduly burdensome guidelines on abortion providers to make access more challenging and expensive. In their analysis of states from 1974 to 2008, Medoff and Dennis found that Republican institutional control of the state legislature and executive branch was most positively associated with states enacting TRAP laws, not necessarily religion or public anti-abortion attitudes. This finding is consistent with the information shared in Table 3.1, where the most restrictive states in terms of abortion access are controlled by Republican governments. Essentially, Medoff and Dennis (2011), similarly to Yamane and Oldmixon (2006), argue that abortion is not just about morality politics and that it may not even be the biggest factor in influencing policy. Medoff and Dennis argue that a state legislator's vote on abortion is merely made to mirror their own abortion preferences rather than a median voter and that the enactment of TRAP laws are a larger result of partisan political control of state government, not necessarily the level of influence of anti-abortion religious groups. Furthermore, Medoff and Dennis (2011) argue that abortion policy is more of a redistributive issue, meaning the transferring of benefits from one group to another, with both negative and positive spillover effects. For example, such as the negative effect abortion may have on those who believe the procedure represents the taking of an innocent life and that this dynamic makes abortion more of a redistributive issue and not a moral one.

However, it may not be wise to throw the baby out with bathwater and disregard religious influence on abortion policies. For example, when revisiting Yamane's and Oldmixon (2006) discussion on saliency, we can see, even if antidotally, how policy makers' orthodox beliefs may shed light on their abortion related legislative behavior, particularly in the language they use in abortion legislation in conservative states, or the rhetoric they employ when justifying pro-life positions. For example, legislators in Missouri passed an abortion ban in 2019, recognizing "that Almighty God is the author of life" (Missouri House Bill 2285). And, when looking at arguments used in testimony during South Carolina's legislative hearings on the state's six-week abortion ban (also referred to as a fetal heartbeat ban), Lambert et al. (2023) found that while religious rhetoric was used sparingly across testimonies, some pro-life proponents did rely on their evangelical Christian beliefs as the basis of their moral arguments about the value and definition of human life, describing life as "sacred" and having "God-given value and dignity of all human life" (pp. 6–7).

Furthermore, several of the states with the most restrictive abortion policies noted in Table 3.1, Louisiana, North Dakota, and Tennessee, also state statutorily that life begins at conception. And other restrictive states, such as Arkansas, Kentucky, Missouri, and Oklahoma, have passed laws declaring life starts at fertilization. Some scholars argue that the position that life begins at conception or fertilization tends to be held as religious belief by some evangelical Protestants and the Catholic Church (Rubenfeld, 1991; Halva-Neubauer and Zeigler, 2010). For example, in a proposed bill out of the Louisiana House of Representatives (again, a state that is 84% Christian, 27% which identify at evangelical Protestant and 26% as Catholic), the "Abolition of Abortion in Louisiana Act of 2022," used religious language to support

TABLE 3.1 States with the Most Restrictive and Protective Access to Abortion in the United States

State	*Abortion Bans*	*Majority Party Control*	*Current Constitutional Amendment*	*Initiatives or Legislation Post-Dobbs*	*Religious Make-up of State*	*Restrictive/ Protective*
AL	Banned unless serious health risk to mother. Medicated abortion included in ban. Physicians can face criminal charges.	Governor: R Senate: R House: R	Amendment 2 (2018): Recognize the sanctity of unborn life and rights of unborn children, including right to life.	No	Christian: 86%, (Evangelical Protestant 49%) Other: 1% Nones: 12%	Most restrictive
AR	Banned unless to save pregnant person's life in a medical emergency. Medicated abortion included in ban. Physicians can face criminal charges.	Governor: R Senate: R House: R	No	Yes. Efforts to advance "Arkansas Abortion Amendment of 2024," to ease restriction on access in case of rape, incest, fatal fetal anomaly, or good-faith medical judgment. Effective "trigger ban," passed in 2019.	Christian: 79%, (Evangelical Protestant 46%) Other: 3% Nones: 18%	Most restrictive

(*Continued*)

TABLE 3.1 (Continued)

State	*Abortion Bans*	*Majority Party Control*	*Current Constitutional Amendment*	*Initiatives or Legislation Post-Dobbs*	*Religious Make-up of State*	*Restrictive/ Protective*
ID	Banned unless to prevent death of pregnant woman, best opportunity for unborn child to survive, rape, or incest. Medicated abortion included in ban. Physicians can face criminal charges.	Governor: R Senate: R House: R	No	No, but effective "trigger ban," passed in 2020, enforcing heartbeat act prohibiting abortion at detection took effect after Dobbs.	Christian: 67%, (Evangelical Protestant 21%) Other: 6% Nones: 27%	Most restrictive
IN	Banned unless to prevent serious health risk of pregnant woman or save her life, lethal fetal anomaly, rape, or incest. Medicated abortion included in ban. Physicians can face criminal charges.	Governor: R Senate: R House: R	No	No, but Senate Bill 1 was the first state to implement legislation on abortion restrictions took effect after Dobbs.	Christian: 72%, (Evangelical Protestant 31%) Other: 2% Nones: 26%	Most restrictive
KY	Banned unless to save the life of a pregnant person or prevent serious risk to pregnant person's physical health. Medicated abortion included in ban. Physicians can face criminal charges.	Governor: D Senate: R House: R	No	No, effective "trigger ban," passed in 2019, prohibiting all abortions upon the overturning of *Roe v. Wade*, enforcing heartbeat act prohibiting abortion at detection took effect after Dobbs.	Christian: 76%, (Evangelical Protestant 49%) Other: 2% Nones: 22%	Most restrictive

State	Abortion Bans	Majority Party Control	Current Constitutional Amendment	Initiatives or Legislation Post-Dobbs	Religious Make-up of State	Restrictive/ Protective
LA	Banned unless necessary to prevent death, substantial risk of death, or permanent impairment of a life-sustaining organ of a pregnant woman. Medicated abortion included in ban. Physicians can face criminal charges.	Governor: R Senate: R House: R	Amendment 1 (2020): Adding a sentence of Louisiana Declaration of Rights, protecting human life, not protecting right to or funding of abortion.	No, effective "trigger ban," passed in 2006, prohibiting all abortions upon the overturning of *Roe v. Wade*, enforcing heartbeat act prohibiting abortion at detection took effect after Dobbs.	Christian: 84%, (Evangelical Protestant 27%) Other: 3% Nones: 13%	Most restrictive
MO	Banned unless medical emergency, requires abortion provider to give an affirmative defense. Medicated abortion included in ban. Physicians can face criminal charges.	Governor: R Senate: R House: R	No	Yes. Efforts to advance "Missouri Right to Reproductive Freedom Amendment," to protect abortion and reproductive rights up until fetal viability, with exceptions after this point to protect life and health of pregnant woman.	Christian: 77%, (Evangelical Protestant 36%) Other: 3% Nones: 20%	Most restrictive

(*Continued*)

TABLE 3.1 (Continued)

State	*Abortion Bans*	*Majority Party Control*	*Current Constitutional Amendment*	*Initiatives or Legislation Post-Dobbs*	*Religious Make-up of State*	*Restrictive/ Protective*
MS	Banned unless where necessary to preserve the life of the mother or cases of rape. Medicated abortion included in ban. Physicians can face criminal charges.	Governor: R Senate: R House: R	No	No, but effective "trigger ban" per 2006 law took effect after Dobbs. Yes. Efforts to advance ballot initiative that would block changes to current abortion law.	Christian: 83%, (Evangelical Protestant 41%) Other: 3% Nones: 14%	Most restrictive
ND	Banned unless to prevent the death or a serious health risk to the pregnant person, or in cases of rape or incest within the six weeks of pregnancy. Medicated abortion included in ban. Physicians can face criminal charges.	Governor: R Senate: R House: R	No	No	Christian: 77%, (Evangelical Protestant 36%) Other: 3% Nones: 20%	Most restrictive

State	Abortion Bans	Majority Party Control	Current Constitutional Amendment	Initiatives or Legislation Post-Dobbs	Religious Make-up of State	Restrictive/ Protective
OK	Illegal in most cases unless necessary to preserve life of the pregnant woman. State Supreme Court stroked down two state laws banning abortion in May 2023. Medicated abortion included in ban. Physicians can face criminal charges.	Governor: R Senate: R House: R	No	No	Christian: 79%, (Evangelical Protestant 47%) Other: 3% Nones: 18%	Most restrictive
SC	Banned except in cases of medical emergency, rape, incest, or fetal anomalies. Legislation includes a fetal heartbeat protection at six weeks. Medicated abortion included in ban. Physicians can face criminal charges.	Governor: R Senate: R House: R	No	No	Christian: 78%, (Evangelical Protestant 35%) Other: 3% Nones: 19%	Most restrictive
SD	Banned except in cases to preserve the life of the mother. Medicated abortion included in ban Physicians can face criminal charges.	Governor: R Senate: R House: R		No, but effective "trigger ban," passed in 2005 took effect after Dobbs.	Christian: 79%, (Evangelical Protestant 25%) Other: 3% Nones: 18%	Most restrictive

(Continued)

TABLE 3.1 (Continued)

State	*Abortion Bans*	*Majority Party Control*	*Current Constitutional Amendment*	*Initiatives or Legislation Post-Dobbs*	*Religious Make-up of State*	*Restrictive/ Protective*
TN	Banned with exception to prevent the death of pregnant woman or prevent serious risk or substantial and irreversible impairment of major bodily function. Medicated abortion included in ban. Physicians can face criminal charges.	Governor: R Senate: R House: R	Amendment 1: Added language to the Constitution, stating nothing secures or protects a right to abortion or requires funding for an abortion.	No, but effective "trigger ban," passed in 2019 took effect after Dobbs.	Christian: 81%, (Evangelical Protestant 52%) Other: 5% Nones: 14%	Most restrictive
TX	Banned with exception of great risk of the pregnant female's death; or serious risk of substantial impairment of major bodily function of the pregnant woman. Medicated abortion included in ban. Physicians can face criminal charges.	Governor: R Senate: R House: R	No	No, but effective "trigger ban" per 2021 law took effect after Dobbs.	Christian: 77%, (Evangelical Protestant 31%) Other: 5% Nones: 18%	Most restrictive
WV	Banned with exception if necessary to save life of mother or fetus, fetus is not viable, or ectopic pregnancy. Medicated abortion included in ban. Physicians can face criminal charges.	Governor: R Senate: R House: R	Amendment 1 (2018): Stating nothing in the Constitution secures a right to an abortion or requires funding for an abortion.	No	Christian: 78%, (Evangelical Protestant 39%) Other: 4% Nones: 18%	Most restrictive

State	*Abortion Bans*	*Majority Party Control*	*Current Constitutional Amendment*	*Initiatives or Legislation Post-Dobbs*	*Religious Make-up of State*	*Restrictive/ Protective*
OR	No legal restrictions and access to medication abortion by mail available.	Governor: D Senate: D House: D	No	House Bill 2002, passed in 2023, protecting abortion as a fundamental right.	Christian: 61%, (Evangelical Protestant 29%) Other: 8% Nones: 31%	Most protective
VT	No legal restrictions and access to medication abortion by mail available.	Governor: R Senate: D House: D	Proposal 5 (2022), added language to Constitution enshrining right to personal reproductive liberty.	Yes. Proposal 5, November 8, 2022, approved.	Christian: 54%, (Evangelical Protestant 11%) Other: 9% Nones: 37%	Most protective
CA	Legal right to abortion through viability, no residency, and access to medication abortion by mail available.	Governor: D Senate: D House: D	Proposition 1, Right to Reproductive Freedom (2022), added language to constitution prohibiting state from interfering with or denying an individual reproductive freedom.	Yes. Proposition 1, November 8, 2022, approved.	Christian: 63%, (Evangelical Protestant 20%) Other: 10% Nones: 27%	Very protective

(*Continued*)

TABLE 3.1 (Continued)

State	*Abortion Bans*	*Majority Party Control*	*Current Constitutional Amendment*	*Initiatives or Legislation Post-Dobbs*	*Religious Make-up of State*	*Restrictive/ Protective*
MD	Legal right to abortion through viability and access to medication abortion by mail available.	Governor: D Senate: D House: D	Advanced to voters for 2024 election.	Yes. Right to Reproductive Freedom Amendment on November 5, 2024, ballot.	Christian: 69%, (Evangelical Protestant 18%) Other: 8% Nones: 23%	Very protective
MN	Legal right to abortion through viability and access to medication abortion by mail available.	Governor: D Senate: D House: D	No, but in 1995 in Doe v. Gomez, the state Supreme Court found state constitution guarantees the right to terminate a pregnancy.	Yes. In 2023, the state legislature passed the PRO Act codifying an individual right to reproductive health care, repealed twenty-four-hour waiting period, and the Reproductive Defense Act protecting providers and patients from civil and criminal penalties for abortion.	Christian: 70%, (Evangelical Protestant 15%) Other: 7% Nones: 23%	Very protective

State	*Abortion Bans*	*Majority Party Control*	*Current Constitutional Amendment*	*Initiatives or Legislation Post-Dobbs*	*Religious Make-up of State*	*Restrictive/ Protective*
NJ	No statutory limitation on abortion, provides for late term access, and medication abortion by mail available.	Governor: D Senate: D House: D	No	Yes. In 2023, the state legislature passed protections mandating some health insurers to cover abortion care, permitting birth control without a prescription, and banning extradition of people who receive or perform abortions in the state.	Christian: 67%, (Evangelical Protestant 13%) Other: 15% Nones: 18%	Very protective
NM	No statutory limitation on abortion, provides for late term access, and medication abortion by mail available.	Governor: D Senate: D House: D	No	Yes. In 2023, the state legislature passed a law prohibiting local municipalities and other public entities from intervening in an individual's access to reproductive care.	Christian: 76%, (Evangelical Protestant 21%) Other: 5% Nones: 19%	Very protective

(*Continued*)

TABLE 3.1 (Continued)

State	*Abortion Bans*	*Majority Party Control*	*Current Constitutional Amendment*	*Initiatives or Legislation Post-Dobbs*	*Religious Make-up of State*	*Restrictive/ Protective*
NY	Legal right to abortion through viability and access to medication abortion by mail available.	Governor: D Senate: D House: D	Advanced to voters in the 2024 election.	Equal Rights Amendment on the 2024 state ballot to prohibition discrimination by the government based on pregnancy and pregnancy outcomes and protects a person's reproductive autonomy.	Christian: 60%, (Evangelical Protestant 10%) Other: 13% Nones: 27%	Very protective

Note: All citations for the information presented in the table are listed on the reference page their pro-life position, acknowledging "the sanctity of innocent human life, created in the image of God, which should be equally protected from fertilization to natural death" (Louisiana House Bill No. 813, 2022). Though the bill did not ultimately become law (some argue due to it classifying abortion as homicide, which both prominent abortion rights groups and anti-abortion organizations argue went too far), this language is part of the personhood movement to protect the lives of the unborn, treating them legally as if they were a child. Some of the strongest personhood movements are taking place in conservative states, such as Alabama, Mississippi, Oklahoma, and South Carolina (Kutz, 2022; NPR, 2023).

However, recently, the personhood movement has been causing challenges for pro-life advocates, as it may threaten couples trying to become parents through in vitro fertilization (IVF). For example, the Alabama Supreme Court on February 26, 2024, handed down a ruling in favor of three parents (plaintiffs) suing a reproductive medical clinic for wrongful death due to their embryos being destroyed. The incident occurred when a patient at the hospital where the clinic was located entered the fertility center through an unsecured entrance, removed several embryos, dropped them on the floor, and killed them when the patient's hand was freeze-burned due to subzero storage temperatures. The Alabama Supreme Court ruled that the state's "Wrongful Death of a Minor Act," which permits parents of deceased children to recover punitive damages for their child's death applies to "extrauterine children-that is, unborn children who are located outside of a biological uterus at the time they are killed" *(James LePage and Emily LePage et. al. v. The Center for Reproductive Medicine, P.C. and Mobile Infirmary Association d/b/a Mobile Infirmary Medical Center,* 2024, pp. 2–5). Since the ruling, some Republicans have stressed concerns about what this may mean for embryos that can be destroyed in the IVF process and worried that the procedure may become less available since people could be sued for destroying an embryo (Terkel et al., 2024). For instance, Member of Congress, Johnson (Republican from Louisiana and the Speaker of the House during the writing of this chapter) stated he supported IVF treatments and that it is "something that's blessed a lot of families who have problems with fertility" (Alfaro, 2024, para. 8). However, as the *Washington Post* reported in the aftermath of the Alabama's Supreme Court decision, some

Republican members of Congress who voiced their support for IVF have also signed on to congressional proposals, such as the "Life at Conception Act" (*Id.* at para. 3). The Act provides no provisions or protections for the IVF process and seeks to "implement equal protection for the right to life of each born and preborn human person," and states that a "human person" and "human being" includes "each and every member of the species homo sapiens at all stages of life, including the moment of fertilization, cloning, or other moment at which an individual member of the human species comes into being" (H. R. 431, 2023). Moreover, "fetal personhood" acts at both the state and national level threaten the use of mifepristone since the drug is used to terminate pregnancy up to seventy days of gestation. Overall, abortion rights activists argue that pro-life strategists are connecting traditional forms of abortion, self-managed abortion, and IVF through the concept of fetal personhood via their rhetoric, legislative language, and litigation to further restrict reproductive rights, particularly in a post-*Dobbs* America (Talukder, 2024).

The case surrounding Kate Cox, a woman out of Dallas, TX, who sought an abortion of a non-viable pregnancy, is another instance that may pose future challenges for the pro-life movement as restrictions are challenged in conservative states. In December 2023, Cox filed a lawsuit against the state of Texas, seeking a temporary restraining order and permanent injunction to stop Texas' trigger pre-*Roe* abortion ban. Cox, who was twenty weeks pregnant at the time of filing, had been in and out of the emergency room for severe cramping and unidentifiable fluid leaks. Ultrasound test suggested her pregnancy was not likely to conclude with a healthy baby and because Cox had two prior cesarean births, proceeding with the pregnancy put her at "high risk for severe complications threatening her life and future fertility" (*Kate Cox; Justin Cox; and Damla Karsan, M.D. v. 3* et al. 2023). The Travis County District Court ruled that neither the Coxs nor their OBGYN should be held criminally or civilly responsible for terminating her pregnancy. Upon filing an emergency petition, Attorney General Ken Paxton asked the state Supreme Court to overturn the lower court's ruling. Paxton also threatened legal action against Cox or any doctor who performed her abortion in the state. In the interim of the state Supreme Court's deliberation on the case, Cox's lawyers shared that her condition was deteriorating and she had left the state to have an abortion. Shortly after, the Texas Supreme Court issued a ruling, overturning the temporary restraining order, holding that Cox's case did not meet the heightened risk to the life of the mother exception of the state's abortion law (Klibanoff, 2023; Basu, 2023).

Interestingly, religious language or beliefs have not just been used by conservative groups in states to support their position on abortion. For example, some members of the Jewish faith in Indiana filed a lawsuit against the medical licensing board, arguing the state is violating the Indiana Religious Freedom Restoration Act because (1) not all adherents of faith groups believe human life begins at conception; (2) that under Jewish law a fetus is not considered a living person until birth; (3) according to Rabbinic tradition, an embryo is considered "mere water" prior to the fortieth day of gestation; and (4) a fetus under the Jewish faith is considered a physical part of a woman's body and does not possess independent life or rights until birth (*Anonymous Plaintiffs 1–5, Hoosiers Jews for Choice v. The Individual Members of the Medical Licensing Board of Indiana et al.*, 2022). In December 2022, the trial court granted the plaintiffs, Hoosiers Jews for Choice, a preliminary injunction prohibiting enforcement against them of the abortion ban while the case proceeds. This injunction was appealed by the state, and the Indiana Court of Appeals heard oral arguments on the matter in December 2023 (Americans United, 2023). In April 2024, the appellate court handed down a ruling agreeing with the lower court that the plaintiffs' religious objection provided them an exemption from the state's near-total abortion ban. However, the judicial panel left open the ability for the ruling to be challenged at the state's Supreme Court (Volmert, 2024).

Furthermore, like Indiana, Kentucky also has a "Religious Freedom Restoration Act, KRS §446.350," which prohibits the government from substantially burdening an individual's freedom of religion. The act grants the right for a person to act or refuse to act "in a manner motivated by a sincerely held religious belief," unless the government provides by clear and convincing evidence that it has a compelling state interest to infringe on the specific act or refusal and does so in a manner that is least restrictive to further the government's interest. Under this statute, three Jewish women in 2023 sued the state, arguing the abortion law, which states life begins at conception, was opposed to Jewish teaching that life begins at birth. The plaintiffs argue that Kentucky's laws on abortion are "Christian in origin." Kentucky Attorney General, Daniel Cameron, argued that the Religious Freedom Restoration Act did not apply in this case because abortion is not a religious practice (Watkins, 2023). Cameron's position harkens back to Medoff and Dennis (2011) and Yamane and Oldmixon (2006) argument about abortion policy being more related to partisan politics more morality politics, or it can also be an example of partisan politicians employing religion when it works in the favor (i.e., Cameron defending the use of the Act over COVID-19 restrictions on houses of worship but arguing against Jewish women invoking the statute as religious grounds to protect access to abortion) Cameron's about face on the Religious Freedom Restoration Act is also an interesting take considering Lewis' (2017) work, which argues that conservatives have shifted from morality politics on issues like abortion toward an argument centered on individual rights, particularly in their legal arguments. Here, it seems that this narrative of using a law like Indiana's Religious Freedom Restoration Act to protect individual members of the Jewish faith from having to go along with the state's restrictive abortion policies does not cut if for Cameron. Perhaps it is that conservatives favor individual rights arguments for Christians but not other faiths. In the end, the plaintiffs were not able to secure a victory, due the Circuit Court in Jefferson County ruling the parties did not have legal standing, an order in line with a state Supreme Court ruling that Planned Parenthood and EMW Women's Surgical Center in Louisville lacked legal standing to challenge the state's abortion ban on behalf of patients (Watkins, 2023).

As previously discussed, the fight between Red versus Blue states over abortion access in the aftermath of the *Dobbs* decision is also playing out over which states permit the dispensing of mifepristone by mail or retail locations, such as Walgreens and CVS. Conservative states (some noted as the most restrictive in Table 3.1) such as Alabama, Alaska, Arkansas, Florida, Georgia, Indiana, Iowa, Kentucky, Louisiana, Mississippi, Montana, North Dakota, Ohio, Oklahoma, South Carolina, South Dakota, Texas, Utah, and West Virginia have threatened legal action against drugstores, such as Walgreens if they proceed to offer the abortion pill at their stores in their respective states. Feeling the pressure from these states, Walgreens, the second largest pharmacy chain in the country, announced in early 2023 that it would not provide the medication in these states but would do so in jurisdictions where it is legal and feasible (Gliadkovskaya, 2023). As a reaction to Walgreens stating they would not provide the abortion pill in these conservative states, leaders of Blue states who are strongly protecting abortion access, such as Governor Gavin Newsom of California, threaten to halt business relations with the corporation that the state contracts with through their Medicaid program. Upon Walgreen's taking this position, Newsom posted on social media, "California won't be doing business with @walgreens—or any company that cowers to the extremists and puts women's lives at risk. We're done" (Krieg and Meyersohn, 2023).

In the aftermath of Newsom's comments, Walgreens stated that their position is to complete the certification process to dispense the medication through the Food and Drug Administration (FDA) and then proceed providing the abortion pill where it is legally permissible, including California. Because California is legally bound under federal law to pay Walgreens through Medi-Cal, which permits patients to obtain medications at approved pharmacies, the Newsom Administration has since confirmed it will continue to comply with the existing agreement. Moreover, in March 2024, both CVS and Walgreens confirmed that they have been certified by the FDA to dispense mifepristone and plan to roll out the medication in a handful of states; however, they will not provide the pill via mail (Belluck, 2024). Walgreens was certified to carry mifepristone under the manufacturer, Danco Laboratories, which, as discussed in Chapter 2, also filed a lawsuit against the Alliance of Hippocratic Medicine in their effort to get the FDA's approval pulled from the abortion pill.

However, some restrictive states are also preventing access to mifepristone by implementing legislation that criminalizes the drug. For example, on May 21, 2024, the Louisiana House of Representatives passed an amendment to Senate Bill 276, criminalizing the possession of mifepristone and misoprostol without a prescription (Louisiana Senate Bill No. 276, 2024). The bill is expected to be sent back to the state Senate for a concurring vote and signed into law by Republican Governor Jeff Landry. Before the House passed this bill, Louisiana already deemed abortion pills illegal through mail (Weixel, 2024). However, shield laws in Blue states, such as those in California, protect providers and patients who assist others in accessing abortion services and related medication from out-of-state legal action. These shield laws have helped prescribers circumvent state bans by prescribing medicated abortion through telehealth services (California Senate Bill 345, 2023). The Louisiana bill marks the first time a state has categorized abortion drugs as controlled substances. This move threatens access to medication via out-of-state telehealth providers because, to prescribe a controlled substance in Louisiana, doctors need a special license. The state then tracks the patient, physician, and pharmacy involved in filling each prescription under this category of drugs (Weixel, 2024).

The fight between Red and Blue states on the abortion pill being dispensed via the country's largest pharmacies and the movement to criminalize mifepristone are examples of how political polarizing the issue is across the country. The dynamics of federalism further complicate the issue, as the *Dobb's* decision has now left the matter to the states to decide. As Associate Supreme Court Justice Brett Kavanaugh stated in his concurring opinion in *Dobbs*, "The Constitution is therefore neither pro-life nor pro-choice. The Constitution is neutral and leaves the issue for the people and their elected representatives to resolve through the democratic process in States or Congress…" (*Dobbs v. Jackson Women's Health Organization,* 2022). Though each state has its own character, what makes a state generally Blue or Red is its consistent ideological positioning on certain issues (i.e., abortion) or preferences for political candidates and leadership (voting more strongly for Democrats or Republicans). Bearing this in mind, scholars have shown that governors and state legislatures' positions on abortion can be strongly influenced by their constituents' ideological positions. This helps to explain why Governor Gavin Newsom of California (a state where 47% of voters identify as Democrat, 24% as Republican, 23% as Decline to State, and over 70% of the electorate recently voted to protect abortion rights) has a different position on abortion than his counterpart from Wyoming, Governor Mark Gordon (a state where 57% voters identify as Republican and only 20% of Republicans agree that abortion is a personal choice), who in March 2023, signed legislation banning the abortion pill (Kahane, 1994; University of Wyoming, 2022; Gruver, 2023; Castle Work, 2024).

Heading into the 2024 General Election, several states either passed legislation to enshrine the right to abortion access into their state laws or constitutions, while others have these issues on their ballots, such as Maryland and New York. In addition to these legislative efforts, some of these states, like California, a leader in the reproductive rights movement, have passed legislation protecting abortion providers who service out-of-state patients looking to terminate their pregnancies, such as Senate Bill 345, which strengthen protections for providers against enforcement of state laws that criminalize or limit reproductive services. As well as expanding the type of providers who can perform abortion services, such as Senate Bill 385, which allows physician assistants to provide abortion care (Office of Governor Gavin Newsom, 2023). Furthermore, in the aftermath of some state court decisions to uphold outdated laws on abortion, such as in Arizona (which is discussed in the next chapter), Governor Gavin Newsom has signed a safe harbor bill, allowing doctors from the state to lawfully perform abortions on their patients in California through the end of November (California Senate Bill 233, 2024). In promoting his execution of the bill, Governor Newsom stated, "California will remain a safe harbor, ready to defend abortion access because we value women's health and trust women to make the most intimate decisions about their bodies, health, and futures" (Office of Governor Newsom, 2024).

Yet, some conservative states, such as Kansas, continue to double down on abortion restrictions despite voters rejecting a proposed state constitutional amendment that would have stated there was no right to an abortion in the state (Lysen et al., 2022). For example, Kansas' House Bill 2749, which was passed by overriding a veto from Governor Laura Kelly in May 2024, requires health care providers to question patients looking to procure an abortion to disclose their reasons for seeking the procedure. The law is set to take effect on July 1, 2024, and several Kansas abortion providers have filed a legal challenge against the bill, hoping to stay the implementation of the act (Kansas House Bill 2749, 2024; Center for Reproductive Rights, 2024).

The *Dobbs* decision will continue to have a lasting impact on how states deal with the issue of abortion for years, if not decades, to come. Though Justice Kavanaugh stated in his concurring opinion that "Today's decision therefore does not prevent numerous State that readily allow abortion from continuing to readily allow abortion," the decision has set forth an even more complex system throughout of the states in assessing where the procedure is legal, where it is not, and under what circumstances one can or cannot procure an abortion. This dynamic has caused both "Red" and "Blue" states to double down on their abortion positions, making it a key issue for future elections.

Moreover, the aftermath of the *Dobbs* decision and how Blue v. Red states have responded to access to abortion in their respective states has real human consequences. Some researchers have voiced concerned for the potential increase of intimate partner violence and rape in the aftermath of the *Dobbs* decision, particular in states that have limited access to the procedure or banned it altogether. For example, research has found that intimate partner sexual violence is a consistent and strong factor in producing unintended pregnancies (Pallitto et al., 2013; Morcek and Posey, 2022). Dickman et al. (2024) found that in the aftermath of *Dobbs*, the fourteen immediate states that outlawed abortion showed an increase in rape related pregnancies, and this pattern held in states with rape exceptions. Nguyen et al. (2022) point out that these unintended pregnancies in a post-*Dobbs* America are more likely to occur among women who are racial and ethnic minorities, and on the lower end of the socioeconomic scale. Therefore, hostile and restrictive abortion policies will continue to impact already marginalized communities. For instance, Nguyen et al. (2022) report that females with a household income under $7,500 are already twelve times more likely to report incidences of sexual assault or rape than women with annual household incomes exceeding $75,000.00 and that nearly a quarter of black women and over a quarter of indigenous women are raped during their lifetimes.

In grappling with the consequences of the *Dobbs* decision, it seems that Cohen et al. (2023) have accurately predicted that not only would the ruling create a new era of abortion laws and points of restriction and access, but that state borders and jurisdiction would become the primary focus of the abortion battle. *Roe* and *Casey* gave some sense of national uniformity to abortion law. However, *Dobbs* has created a hodgepodge system across the country, ensuring legal battles between states on the issue continue as these entities navigate telehealth abortion services, medicated abortion by mail, and other online services granting access to reproductive health services.

Overall, abortion is a multifaceted issue, where elements of religion and morality politics create an undertone and framing of the debate but take a back seat to partisan political and ideological positions and influence on the issue. Regardless, all these elements create a passionate debate on abortion with varying policies from state to state. The next chapter will continue to touch on how religious groups, conservatives, as well as pro-choice groups, strategized for the 2024 election and beyond, as well as provide insight into the Supreme Court's ruling on the *Food and Drug Administration v. Alliance for Hippocratic Medicine* (2024).

References

Abortion: Concealing Death of Child. *Chapter 32 § 861. Oklahoma State Legislature*. Available at: https://govt.westlaw.com/okjc/Document/N8BCFBDF0C76A11DB8F04FB3E68C8F4C5?viewType=FullText&originationContext=documenttoc&transitionType=CategoryPageItem&contextData=(sc.Default)&bhcp=1 (Accessed: 23 February 2024).

Abortion Control Act. *Chapter 14002.1-01-09. North Dakota Legislature*. Available at: chrome-extension://efaidnbmnnnibpcajpcglclefindmkaj/https://ndlegis.gov/cencode/t14c02-1.pdf (Accessed: 23 February 2024).

Abortion Finder. *Abortion in Kentucky*. Available at: https://www.abortionfinder.org/abortion-guides-by-state/abortion-in-kentucky (Accessed: 16 February 2024).

Alabama Human Life Protection Act. Ala. Code § 26-23H-4. *Alabama State Legislature*. Available at: https://law.justia.com/codes/alabama/2022/title-26/chapter-23h/ (Accessed: 13 February 2024).

Alfaro, M. (2024) 'Republicans Who Say They Support IVF Backed a Bill Protecting Life 'At Conception', *The Washington Post*, 25 February. Available at https://www.washingtonpost.com/politics/2024/02/25/ivf-republicans-legislation/ (Accessed: 2 April 2024).

American Civil Liberties Union (2024) *New York Needs An Equal Rights Amendment*. Available at: https://www.nyclu.org/en/campaigns/new-york-needs-equal-rights-amendment (Accessed: 8 March 2024).

Americans United for the Separation of Church and State (2023) *Individual Members of the Medical Licensing Board of Indiana v. Anonymous Plaintiff 1*. Available at: https://www.au.org/how-we-protect-religious-freedom/legal-cases/cases/individual-members-of-the-medical-licensing-board-of-indiana-v-anonymous-plaintiff-1/ (Accessed: 2 April 2024).

Anonymous Plaintiffs 1–5, Hoosier Jews for Choice v. The Individual Members of the Medical Licensing Board of Indiana, et al. (2023) 'Marion Superior Court, case 49D01–2209-PL-031056', *American Civil Liberties Union*. Available at: https://www.aclu-in.org/sites/default/files/field_documents/complaint_to_file.pdf (Accessed: 2 April 2024).

Arkansas Abortion Amendment of 2024. Available at: https://arkansasadvocate.com/wp-content/uploads/2024/01/Abortion-Amendment-of-2024.pdf (Accessed: 13 February 2024).

Ballotpedia (2018) *Alabama Amendment 2, State Abortion Policy Amendment*. Available at: https://ballotpedia.org/Alabama_Amendment_2,_State_Abortion_Policy_Amendment_(2018) (Accessed: 09 February 2024).

Ballotpedia (2020) *Louisiana Amendment 1, No Right to Abortion in Constitution Amendment*. Available at: https://ballotpedia.org/

Louisiana_Amendment_1,_No_Right_to_Abortion_in_Constitution_Amendment_(2020) (Accessed: 18 February 2024).

Ballotpedia (2022) *California Proposition 1, Right to Reproductive Freedom Amendment*. Available at: https://www5.open.ac.uk/library/referencing-and-plagiarism/quick-guide-to-harvard-referencing-cite-them-right#s1 (Accessed: 28 February 2024).

Ballotpedia (2022) *Vermont Proposal 5, Right to Personal Reproductive Autonomy Amendment*. Available at: https://ballotpedia.org/Vermont_Proposal_5,_Right_to_Personal_Reproductive_Autonomy_Amendment_(2022) (Accessed: 28 February 2024).

Ballotpedia (2024) *Party Control of Alabama State Government*. Available at: https://ballotpedia.org/Party_control_of_Alabama_state_government (Accessed: 09 February 2024).

Ballotpedia (2024) *Party Control of Arizona State Government*. Available at: https://ballotpedia.org/Party_control_of_Arizona_state_government (Accessed: 10 April 2024).

Ballotpedia (2024) *Party Control of Arkansas State Government*. Available at: https://ballotpedia.org/Party_control_of_Arkansas_state_government (Accessed: 13 February 2024).

Ballotpedia (2024) *Party Control of California State Government*. Available at: https://ballotpedia.org/Party_control_of_California_state_government (Accessed: 28 February 2024).

Ballotpedia (2024) *Party Control of Idaho State Government*. Available at: https://ballotpedia.org/Party_control_of_Idaho_state_government (Accessed: 13 February 2024).

Ballotpedia (2024) *Party Control of Louisiana State Government*. Available at: https://ballotpedia.org/Party_control_of_Louisiana_state_government (Accessed: 18 February 2024).

Ballotpedia (2024) *Party Control of Missouri State Government*. Available at: https://ballotpedia.org/Party_control_of_Missouri_state_government (Accessed: 18 February 2024).

Ballotpedia (2024) *Party Control of Mississippi State Government*. Available at: https://ballotpedia.org/Party_control_of_Mississippi_state_government (Accessed: 18 February 2024).

Ballotpedia (2024) *Party Control of North Dakota State Government*. Available at: https://ballotpedia.org/Party_control_of_North_Dakota_state_government (Accessed: 23 February 2024).

Ballotpedia (2024) *Party Control of Maryland State Government*. Available at: https://ballotpedia.org/Party_control_of_Maryland_state_government (Accessed: 1 March 2024).

Ballotpedia (2024) *Party Control of Minnesota State Government*. Available at: https://ballotpedia.org/Party_control_of_Minnesota_state_government (Accessed: 1 March 2024).

Ballotpedia (2024) *Party Control of New Jersey State Government*. Available at: https://ballotpedia.org/Party_control_of_New_Jersey_state_government (Accessed: 4 March 2024).

Ballotpedia (2024) *Party Control of New York*. Available at: https://ballotpedia.org/Party_control_of_New_York_state_government (Accessed: 8 March 2024)

Ballotpedia (2024) *Party Control of Oklahoma*. Available at: https://ballotpedia.org/Party_control_of_Oklahoma_state_government (Accessed: 23 February 2024).

Ballotpedia (2024) *Party Control of South Carolina*. Available at: https://ballotpedia.org/Party_control_of_South_Carolina_state_government (Accessed: 23 February 2024).

Ballotpedia (2024) *Party Control of Tennessee*. Available at: https://ballotpedia.org/Party_control_of_Tennessee_state_government (Accessed: 23 February 2024).

Ballotpedia (2024) *Tennessee Amendment 1, No State Constitutional Right to Abortion and Legislative Power to Regulate Abortion Amendment (2014)*. Available at: https://ballotpedia.org/Tennessee_Amendment_1,_No_State_Constitutional_Right_to_Abortion_and_Legislative_Power_to_Regulate_Abortion_Amendment_(2014) (Accessed: 23 February 2024).

Ballotpedia (2024) *West Virginia Amendment 1, No Right to Abortion in Constitution Measure (2018)*. Available at: https://ballotpedia.org/West_Virginia_Amendment_1,_No_Right_to_Abortion_in_Constitution_Measure_(2018) (Accessed: 28 February 2024)

Ballotpedia (2024) *Party Control of Vermont State Government*. Available at: https://ballotpedia.org/Party_control_of_Vermont_state_government (Accessed: 28 February 2024).

Basu, Z. (2023) 'The Inescapable Abortion Campaign', *AXIOS*, 13 December. Available at: https://www.axios.com/2023/12/14/kate-cox-abortion-republicans-2024 (Accessed: 2 April 2024).

Belluck, P. (2024) 'CVS and Walgreens Will Begin Selling Abortion Pills This Month', *New York Times*, 1 March. Available at: https://www.nytimes.com/2024/03/01/health/abortion-pills-cvs-walgreens.html (Accessed: 2 April 2024).

California All. (2024) *Your Legal Right to an Abortion*. Available at: https://abortion.ca.gov/your-rights/your-legal-right-to-an-abortion/index.html (Accessed: 28 February 2024).

Castle Work, M. (2024) 'Even in Bright-Blue California, Abortion is on the Ballot', *The Washington Post*, 07 February. Available at: https://www.washingtonpost.com/politics/2024/02/07/even-bright-blue-california-abortion-is-ballot/ (Accessed: 1 April 2024).

Center for Reproductive Rights (2024) *Kansas Abortion Providers Challenge New Law Forcing Them to Give Patient Information to the State*. Available at: https://reproductiverights.org/kansas-abortion-providers-challenge-new-law-forcing-them-give-patient-information-state/ (Accessed: 28 May 2024).

Cohen, D.S., Donley, G., and Rebouché, R. (2023) 'The New Abortion Battleground', *Columbia Law Review*, 123(1), pp.1–100.

Defense of Life Act. *Idaho State Legislature*. Available at: https://legislature.idaho.gov/statutesrules/idstat/title18/t18ch6/sect18-622/#:~:text=defense%20of%20life%20act.,the%20crime%20of%20criminal%20abortion. (Accessed: 13 February 2024).

Dickman, S., White, K., and Himmelstein, D. (2024) 'Rape-Related Pregnancies in the 14 US States With Total Abortion Bans', *The Journal of the American Medical Association*, 184(3), pp.330–332. Available at: doi:10.1001/jamainternmed.2024.0014

Difilippo, D., and Nieto-Munoz, S. (2023) 'A Year After Dobbs, New Jersey Abortion Rights Advocates Celebrate Wins—But Fear Backsliding', *New Jersey Monitor*, 23 June. Available at: https://newjerseymonitor.com/2023/06/23/a-year-after-dobbs-new-jersey-abortion-rights-advocates-celebrate-wins-but-fear-backsliding/ (Accessed: 4 March 2024).

Dobbs v. Jackson Women's Health Organization, 597 U.S.__(2002)

Edelman, A. (2024) 'Missouri Abortion Rights Groups Launch Effort to Place Constitutional amendment on 2024 Ballot', *NBC News*, 18 January. Available at: https://www.nbcnews.com/politics/2024-election/missouri-abortion-rights-constitutional-amendment-ballot-rcna134371 (Accessed: 18 February 2024).

Fetal Heartbeat and Protection from Abortion Act. (2023) *South Carolina Legislature*. Available at: https://www.scstatehouse.gov/sess125_2023-2024/bills/474.htm (Accessed: 23 February 2024).

FDA v. Alliance for Hippocratic Medicine, 602 U.S.___(2024)

Gliadkovskaya, A. (2023) 'Walgreens Won't Sell Abortion Pills in GOP States After Legal Threats from State Officials; California Won't Renew Contract', *Fierce Healthcare,* 9 March. Available at: https://www.fiercehealthcare.com/regulatory/walgreens-wont-sell-abortion-pills-gop-states-after-threats (Accessed: 2 April 2024).

Gruver, M. (2023) 'Wyoming Governor Signs Measure Prohibiting Abortion Pills', *Associated Press*, 18 March. Available at: https://apnews.com/article/wyoming-medication-abortion-ban-gordon-8120493afa25f7a2d4233192dc612cb3 (Accessed: 2 April 2024).

Guttmacher Institute (2024) *Interactive Map: US Abortion Policies and Access After Roe*. Available at: https://states.guttmacher.org/policies/oregon/abortion-policies (Accessed: 9 February 2024).

Haiar, J. (2023) 'Some South Dakota Abortion Rights Groups Don't Back Ballot Measure to Restore Access', *Stateline*, 11 December. Available at: https://stateline.org/2023/12/11/some-south-dakota-abortion-rights-groups-dont-back-ballot-measure-to-restore-access/#:~:text=The%20U.S.%20

Supreme%20Court%20overturned,the%20life%20of%20the%20mother (Accessed: 23 February 2024).

Halva-Nuebaur, G., and Zeigler, S.L. (2010) 'Promoting Fetal Personhood: The Rhetorical and Legislative Strategies of the Pro-Life Movement after Planned Parenthood v. Casey', *Feminist Formations*, 22(2), pp.101–123. Available at: https://www.jstor.org/stable/40835373 (Accessed: 1 April 2024).

House Bill 7. *New Mexico State Legislature*. Available at: https://www.nmlegis.gov/Legislation/Legislation?Chamber=H&LegType=B&LegNo=7&year=23 (Accessed: 4 March 2024).

House Bill 148. *Kentucky State Legislature*. Available at: https://legiscan.com/KY/bill/HB148/2019 (Accessed: 16 February 2024).

House Bill 813: The Abolition of Abortion in Louisiana Act of 2022. *Louisiana State Legislature*. Available at: https://legis.la.gov/legis/BillInfo.aspx?i=242732 (Accessed: 1 April 2024).

House Bill 1029. *Tennessee State Legislature*. Available at: https://wapp.capitol.tn.gov/apps/BillInfo/default.aspx?BillNumber=HB1029&GA=111 (Accessed: 23 February 2024).

House Bill 1280. *Texas State Legislature*. Available at: https://capitol.texas.gov/tlodocs/87R/billtext/html/HB01280F.htm (Accessed: 23 February 2024).

House Bill 24749: Requiring Medical Care Facilities and Providers to Report Reasons for Each Abortion Performed at Such Facility or by Such Provider the Secretary of Health and Environment. *Kansas State Legislature*. Available at: https://legiscan.com/KS/text/HB2749/id/2975312 (Accessed: 28 May 2024).

House Resolution 431: Life at Conception Act. *United States House of Representatives*. Available at: https://www.congress.gov/bill/118th-congress/house-bill/431/text (Accessed: 2 April 2024).

Indiana Health Code Title 16, Section 34-2-7. *Indiana State Legislature*. Available at: https://codes.findlaw.com/in/title-16-health/in-code-sect-16-34-2-7/ (Accessed: 1 March 2024).

LePage, J., and LePage, E. et al. v. The Center for Reproductive Medicine, P.C. and Mobile Infirmary Association d/b/a Mobile Infirmary Medical Center (2024) 'Supreme Court of Alabama, case SC-2022–0515', *Justia*. Available at: https://law.justia.com/cases/alabama/supreme-court/2024/sc-2022-0579.html (Accessed: 1 April 2024).

Jarecki, J., and Trevellyan, K. (2023) 'Vermonters Can Still Access Abortion Medication Mifepristone, but Future Remains Uncertain', *Vermont Public*, 17 April. Available at: https://www.vermontpublic.org/local-news/2023-04-17/vermonters-can-still-access-abortion-medication-mifepristone-but-future-remains-uncertain (Accessed: 28 February 2024).

Kahane, L.H. (1994) 'Political, Ideological and Economic Determinants of Abortion Positions: An Empirical Analysis of State Legislatures and Governors', *The American Journal of Economics and Sociology*, 53(3), pp.347–360. Available at: https://www.jstor.org/stable/3487299 (Accessed: 1 April 2024).

Kate Cox; Justin Cox; and Damla Karsan, M.D. v. State of Texas et al. (2023) *District Court of Travis County, Texas*. Available at: https://reproductiverights.org/wp-content/uploads/2023/12/Cox-v.-Texas-original-petition-FINAL.pdf (Accessed: 2 April 2024).

Klibanoff, E. (2023) 'Texas Supreme Court Blocks Order Allowing Abortion; Woman Who Sought it Leaves State', *Texas Tribune*, 11 December. Available at: https://www.texastribune.org/2023/12/11/texas-abortion-lawsuit-kate-cox/#:~:text=The%20Texas%20Supreme%20Court%20has,terminate%20her%20non%2Dviable%20pregnancy (Accessed: 2 April 2024).

Krieg, G., and Meyersohn, N. (2023) 'Newsom to Shut Walgreens out of California State Business Following Abortion Pill Decision', *CNN*, 8 March. Available at: https://www.cnn.com/2023/03/07/politics/gavin-newsom-walgreens-california-abortion-drug/index.html (Accessed: 2 April 2024).

Kutz, J. (2022) 'Pushback on Louisiana's Scuttled Abortion Bill Reveals a Limit on How Far Anti-Abortion Groups are Willing to Go', *The 19th*, 13 May. Available at: https://19thnews.org/2022/05/louisiana-law-anti-abortion-group-limits/ (Accessed: 1 April 2024).

Lambert, V.C., Hackworth, E.E., and Billings, D.L. (2023) 'Qualitative Analysis of Anti-Abortion Discourse Used in Arguments for a 6-week Abortion Ban in South Carolina', *Frontiers in Global Women's Health*. Available at: https://pmc.ncbi.nlm.nih.gov/articles/PMC10098009/ (Accessed: 1 April 2024).

Lysen, D., Ziegler, L., and Mesa, B. (2022) 'Voters in Kansas Decide to Keep Abortion Legal in the State, Rejecting an Amendment', *NPR*, 3 August. Available at: https://www.npr.org/sections/2022-live-primary-election-race-results/2022/08/02/1115317596/kansas-voters-abortion-legal-reject-constitutional-amendment (Accessed: 28 May 2024).

Medoff, M., and Dennis, C. (2011) 'TRAP Abortion Laws and Partisan Political Party Control of State Government', *The American Journal of Economics and Sociology*, 70(4), pp.951–973. Available at: https://www.jstor.org/stable/41329170 (Accessed: 1 April 2024).

Minnesota Attorney General (2023) *Know Your Rights to Abortion and Reproductive Healthcare in Minnesota*. Available at: https://www.ag.state.mn.us/abortionrights/ (Accessed: 1 March 2024).

Mississippi Public Health Code Title 41, Section 41-41-45: Abortion Prohibited; Exceptions. *Justia*. Available at: https://law.justia.com/codes/mississippi/title-41/chapter-41/performance-of-abortion-consent/section-41-41-45/ (Accessed: 20 June 2025).

Missouri House Bill No. 2285. *Missouri State Legislature*. Available at: chrome-extension://efaidnbmnnnibpcajpcglclefindmkaj/https://documents.

house.mo.gov/billtracking/bills201/hlrbillspdf/4599H.01I.pdf (Accessed: 1 April 2024).

Morczek, A., and Posey, B.M. (2022) 'Intimate Partner Violence After Dobbs: Implications and Recommendations', *Family & Intimate Partner Violence Quarterly*, 15(2), pp.9–31.

Moseley-Morris, K. (2022) 'Idaho Supreme Court Allows Trigger Law Banning Nearly All Abortions to Take Effect', *Idaho Capital Sun*, 12 August. Available at: https://idahocapitalsun.com/2022/08/12/idaho-supreme-court-allows-trigger-law-banning-nearly-all-abortions-to-take-effect/ (Accessed: 16 February 2024).

Nguyen, D., Bajaj, S.S., Ahmed, D., and Stanford, F.C (2022) 'Protecting Marginalized Women's Mental Health in the post-Dobbs Era', *Proceedings of the National Academy of Sciences of the United States of America*, 119(40). Available at: doi: 10.1073/pnas.2212012119

NPR (2023) *4 States Are Using Fetal Personhood to Put Women Behind Bars*. Available at: https://www.npr.org/2023/08/11/1193393737/4-states-are-using-fetal-personhood-to-put-women-behind-bars (Accessed: 1 April 2024).

Office of Governor Gavin Newsom (2023) *California Expands Access and Protections for Reproductive Health Care,* 27 September. Available at: https://www.gov.ca.gov/2023/09/27/california-expands-access-and-protections-for-reproductive-health-care/abortions/?currentTimeframe=0&sortModel=%7B%22colId%22:%22Location%22,%22sort%22:%22asc%22%7D (Accessed: 2 April 2024).

Office of Governor Gavin Newsom (2024) *Governor Newsom Signs Bill to Protect Abortion Care for Arizona Patients in California*, 23 May. Available at: https://www.gov.ca.gov/2024/05/23/governor-newsom-signs-bill-to-protect-abortion-care-for-arizona-patients-in-california/#:~:text=What%20to%20know%3A%20As%20Arizona,a%20temporary%20basis%20in%20California (Accessed: 28 May 2024).

Oregon Department of Justice (2023) *Spotlight: Reproductive Rights*. Available at: https://www.doj.state.or.us/oregon-department-of-justice/office-of-the-attorney-general/spotlight-reproductive-rights/#:~:text=Oregon%20does%20not%20have%20any,(abortion%20pills)%20by%20mail. (Accessed: 28 February 2024).

Pallitto, C.C., Garcia-Moreno, C., Jansen, H.A., Heise, L., Ellsberg, M., and Watts, C. (2013) Intimate Partner Violence, Abortion, and Unintended Pregnancy: Results from the WHO Multi-country Study on Women's Health and Domestic Violence', *International Journal of Gynecology and Obstetrics*, 120(1), pp.3–9. Available at: https://doi.org/10.1016/j.ijgo.2012.07.003

Pew Research Center (2024) *Religious Landscape Study*. Available at: https://www.pewresearch.org/religion/religious-landscape-study/ (Accessed: 9 February 2024).

Planned Parenthood of Southeastern Pa. v. Casey, 505 U.S. 833 (1992)

Procurement of abortion prohibited--Exception to Preserve Life of Pregnant Female—Felony. *South Dakota State Legislature*. Available at: https://sdlegislature.gov/Statutes/22-17-5.1 (Accessed: 23 February 2024).

Religious Freedom Restoration Act, KRS §446.350. *Kentucky State Legislature*. Available at: https://apps.legislature.ky.gov/law/statutes/statute.aspx?id=42395#:~:text=The%20right%20to%20act%20or,has%20used%20the%20least%20restrictive (Accessed: 5 April 2024).

Revised Statue Title 40, Section 1061: Abortion Prohibition. *Louisiana State Legislature*. Available at: https://legis.la.gov/legis/Law.aspx?d=97020 (Accessed: 18 February 2024).

Revised Statute Section 188.017: Right to Life of the Unborn Child Act. *Missouri State Legislature*. Available at: https://revisor.mo.gov/main/OneSection.aspx?section=188.017 (Accessed: 8 February 2024).

Right to Reproductive Freedom (2024). *Maryland General Assembly*. Available at: https://mgaleg.maryland.gov/mgawebsite/Legislation/Details/HB0705?ys=2023RS (Accessed: 1 March 2024).

Roe v. Wade, 410 U.S. 113 (1973)

Rubenfeld, J. (1991) 'On the Legal Status of the Proposition That "Life Begins at Conception"', *Stanford Law Review*, 43(3), pp.599–635. Available at: https://doi.org/10.2307/1228913

Senate Bill 1 Abortion. *Indiana State Legislature*. Available at: https://iga.in.gov/legislative/2022ss1/bills/senate/1/details (Accessed: 13 February 2024).

Senate Bill 233: Practice of Medicine: Arizona Physicians: Abortions and Abortion-related care for Arizona Patients. *California State Legislature*. Available at: https://legiscan.com/CA/text/SB233/id/2813978 (Accessed: 28 May 2024).

Senate Bill 345: Legally Protected Health Care Activities. *California State Legislature*. Available at: https://legiscan.com/CA/text/SB345/id/2750650 (Accessed: 22 May 2024).

Senate Bill 0745. *Tennessee State Legislature*. Available at: https://wapp.capitol.tn.gov/apps/BillInfo/Default.aspx?BillNumber=SB0745 (Accessed: 28 February 2024).

Tabet, A. (2024) 'Arizona Abortion Rights Amendment Backers Says They've Gathered Signatures Needed for 2024 Ballot', *NBC News*, 2 April 2024. Available at: https://www.nbcnews.com/politics/2024-election/arizona-abortion-rights-amendment-backers-says-gathered-signatures-nee-rcna145922 (Accessed: 10 April 2024).

Talukder, S. (2024) 'How the Alabama IVF Ruling Is Connected to Upcoming Supreme Court Cases on Abortion', *American Progress*, 11 March. Available at: https://www.americanprogress.org/article/how-the-alabama-ivf-ruling-is-connected-to-upcoming-supreme-court-cases-on-abortion/ (Accessed: 2 April 2024).

Terkel, A., Tabet, A., Burns, D., and Brooks, A. (2024) 'Alabama's IVF Ruling Puts Republicans in a Political Bind', *NBC News*, 22 February. Available at: https://www.nbcnews.com/politics/2024-election/alabamas-ivf-ruling-embryos-republican-political-bind-rcna140070 (Accessed: 1 April 2024).

University of Wyoming (2022) *Wyoming Opinion on Abortion Has Changed Little in 20 Years, According to UW Survey*, 30 November. Available at: https://www.uwyo.edu/news/2022/11/wyoming-opinion-on-abortion-has-changed-little-in-20-years-according-to-uw-survey.html (Accessed: 2 April 2024).

Volmert, I. (2024) 'Lawsuit Challenging Indiana Abortion Ban Survives a State Challenge', *Associated Press*, 04 April. Available at: https://apnews.com/article/indiana-appeals-court-religious-freedom-law-abortion-4da0cd6d585e69ede87bea2ee2da2896 (Accessed: 21 May 2024).

Vrbin, T. (2023) 'Arkansas AG Rejects Proposed Ballot Measure to Make Abortion Access a Constitutional Right', *Arkansas Advocate*, 28 November. Available at: https://arkansasadvocate.com/2023/11/28/arkansas-ag-rejects-proposed-ballot-measure-to-make-abortion-access-a-constitutional-right/#:~:text=Abortion%20is%20currently%20illegal%20in,put%20this%20law%20in%20place (Accessed: 13 February 2024).

Wald, K., Owen, D., and Hill, S. (1988) 'Churches as Political Communities', *American Political Science Review*, 82, pp.531–548. Available at: doi:10.2307/1957399

Watkins, M. (2023) 'Judge ends key lawsuit against Kentucky's Near-Total Abortion Ban', *Louisville Public Media*, 28 June. Available at: https://www.americanprogress.org/article/how-the-alabama-ivf-ruling-is-connected-to-upcoming-supreme-court-cases-on-abortion/ (Accessed: 2 April 2024).

Weixel, N. (2024) 'Louisiana House Voted to Criminalized Abortion Pills', *The Bill*, 21 May. Available at: https://thehill.com/policy/healthcare/4678268-louisiana-house-criminalize-abortion-pills/ (Accessed: 22 May 2024).

West Virginia Code 61–2–8. *West Virginia State Legislature*. Available at: https://code.wvlegislature.gov/61-2-8/ (Accessed: 23 February 2024).

Yamane, D., and Oldmixon, E. (2006) 'Religion in the Legislative Arena: Affiliation, Salience, Advocacy, and Public Policymaking', *Legislative Studies Quarterly*, 31(3), pp.433–460. Available at: https://www.jstor.org/stable/40263394

4

ACCESS TO CHEMICAL AND EMERGENCY ABORTION SERVICES POST-*DOBBS*

Since the *Dobbs* decision, over twenty states have banned abortion or restricted the timing of when the procedure can occur earlier than the standard imposed by *Roe v. Wade* (1973). As legal battles and abortion ballot initiative efforts ensue in states across the country, it is sure to place the issue of reproductive rights high on the agenda for the 2024 General Election. In gearing up for the election, both religious and secular groups are looking to influence the political process to get public policies on abortion implemented according to their views.

One factor that played into Donald Trump's electoral success in 2016 was the large support of white evangelicals he garnered, favoring him at 80% to 16% (Pulliam Bailey, 2016). Though losing the 2020 election, Trump enjoyed comparable levels of support among white evangelicals (Newport, 2020). Whitehead et al. (2018) argue that this support came on the heels of a fervor of Christian nationalism, a belief rooted in the Old Testament, linking the American religious experience to the God of Israel and espousing that the nation is founded on Christian beliefs and principles. Whitehead et al. (2018) found in their analysis of the 2017 Baylor Religion Survey, that Christian nationalism was a strong role in predicting votes for Trump and that the former President played into these beliefs and values not because he is exceptionally religious, but his rhetoric on the country's assault on Christianity appealed to those partial to Christian nationalist beliefs. So, what might Christian nationalism have to do with the 2024 election and abortion? Well, the Center for Renewing America (CRA), a conservative think tank headed by Russell Vought, Director of Office of Management and Budget during Trump's first term, is leading a group

DOI: 10.4324/9781032636177-4

of conservatives in preparing for a possible second Trump presidency. Materials drafted by the CRA reference Christian nationalism. And, Vought, who is closely affiliated with Christian nationalist William Wolfe, another former Trump Administration official, promotes an end to abortion and reducing access to contraceptives (Ward and Przybyla, 2024). Moreover, conservative Christians believe that former President Trump delivered on his commitment to pro-life judges with his appointments to the federal courts, including Associate Justices Neil Gorsuch, Brett Kavanaugh, and Amy Coney Barrett at the Supreme Court (Keenan and Pereira, 2020).

As previously noted, one of the ways conservative groups geared up for the 2024 election and beyond is to continue legal challenges against the expansion and availability of abortion. Conservatives, such as Donald Trump, have taken credit for the *Dobbs* decision due to his Supreme Court appointments. However, Trump has also endorsed the patchwork abortion system across the states. His endorsement of each state being able to set abortion policy has frustrated some conservatives who believe more legal battles are to come and wish to see abortion banned across the entire country. However, some analysts argue that the election is about winning for Trump, and since abortion will take up a major portion of the electoral agenda in 2024, he may be reacting to polls that show only one in ten Americans agree that abortion should be illegal in all cases. Some report that Trump has told advisors that he likes the idea of a sixteen-week national abortion ban with the exceptions for rape, incest, and to save the life of the mother, with the objective of trying to strike a balance between abortion restrictionists and more moderate voters (Meyer and Stanley, 2024; Haberman et al., 2024; Peoples, 2024; Mulvihill and Sanders, 2023). Trump is not the only Republican politician who has tossed around the idea of an abortion ban set at a specific number of weeks. For example, Senator Lindsey Graham (R-SC) was one of the first elected officials after *Dobbs* to propose a fifteen-week ban, and Kari Lake, Republican candidate for Arizona Senate, supports similar bans (Kamarck, 2024). Some argue that the bans, particular the push for a federal ban, are a way for the Republicans to craft a unified position that they feel is "moderate," because it leaves abortion on the table at early stages and provides for certain exemptions (such as the health of and safety of the mother and in some cases a rape exception). However, the Biden

Administration argues that conservative abortion bans take away individual freedom and rights and are riddled with radical positions, such as House Speaker Mike Johnson's inability to take a clear position on whether he feels destroying embryos as part of the IVF process is murder (Messerly, 2024).

The Biden Administration demonstrated how high the stakes are on abortion in future elections, as evidenced by Kamala Harris' visit to Planned Parenthood in St. Paul, MN. Minnesota is a state that went to the Democratic Presidential nominee in both 2016 and 2020 (CNN, 2020). Harris's visit was the first time a US Vice President or President ever visited such a facility, signifying the importance of the abortion issue in the current political environment (Halpert, 2024). This visit by the Vice President also served to re-emphasize the Administration's commitment to abortion rights and their task force on reproductive healthcare, the latter of which was established this past year to mark what would have been the 51st Anniversary of *Roe v. Wade* (The White House, 2024a). The taskforce looks to meet, implement, and report on the President's effort to strengthen contraception access, reinforce reproductive healthcare obligations under the Affordable Care Act, educate patients of the rights and obligations for emergency medical treatment, protect access to safe and legal medicated based abortions, and of course, defend the FDA's approval of mifepristone in court (White House, 2024a).

The Biden Administration has promised the American people it would strengthen abortion rights at the federal level. However, the President faces mounting challenges as a complex web of varying laws granting or restricting access to abortion plays out post-*Dobbs* decision. (Korecki et al., 2024). For example, on April 9, 2024, the Arizona Supreme Court evaluated whether the state's statute on gestational limits on abortion, Article 3 § 36–2322, which allows physicians to provide abortions up to fifteen weeks of pregnancy and thereafter only in the incident of medical emergencies, repealed or restricted Arizona Revised Statute, § 13–3603, which prohibits abortion expect in a medical emergency and imposes a felony on persons who perform or assist with the act, subjecting them to fine and/or imprisonment for not more than two years (*Planned Parenthood Arizona, Inc. et al. v. Kristin K. Mayes, Attorney General of the State of Arizona et al.*, 2024, pp. 4–5). The Court concluded that

§ 36–2322 does not create a right or provide independent statutory authority for an abortion; therefore, § 13–3603 was not repealed and abortion was effectively banned in Arizona (*Planned Parenthood Arizona, Inc. et al. v. Kristin K. Mayes, Attorney General of the State of Arizona et al.*, 2024, pp. 4–5). The Arizona State Supreme Court rationalized that, in the absence of the federal constitution right to abortion (which again *Dobbs* held did not exist) and Congress not codifying such a right into federal law, § 13–3603 is enforceable (*Id.* at pp. 5–6). In further justifying its decisions, the Court's majority pointed to Arizona territorial, pre-statehood set of laws, such as the Howell Code, which included "constraints on abortion," as well as a 1901 penal code, "dividing criminality between people who facilitate abortions and women who solicit assistance to procure abortion" (*Id.* at p. 5). Furthermore, the majority also argued that from the time of *Roe v. Wade* in 1973 through the *Dobbs* 2022 decision, the Arizona State Legislature passed numerous restrictions on abortion access and that as a matter of clear statutory interpretation, the latter ruling returned "the authority to regulate abortion…to the people and their elected represented" (*Id.* at p. 6). Overall, the majority held that they must enact judicial restraint because the Arizona legislature has consistently demonstrated efforts to restrict abortion access to the extent permitted by the supremacy clause of the US Constitution and has held this position since 1864 (*Id.* at p. 28). The dissent criticized the majority's reliance for their rationale to ban access to abortion on a set of laws that existed before Arizona became a state in 1912. Moreover, the dissent argued that § 36–2322(b) was not ambiguous and that nothing in its language states that abortion accessibility in the state is dependent on *Roe's* continued enforceability and nor does language in the statute suggest it would be rendered inoperative if the Supreme Court of the United States overturned *Roe* (*Id.* at p. 33).

In the aftermath of the ruling, Democrats blamed former President Donald Trump and Republicans for their influence on abortion bans across the country, trying to edge out political advantage on the issue ahead of the 2024 Presidential Election (Cooper, 2024). Heading into the last midterm election cycle in 2022, most Arizona voters (87%) said they wanted abortion to remain legal in either all or some cases (Davis-Young, 2022). And, according to a national survey conducted by Data for Progress, when asking likely voters about the Arizona Supreme Court decision to uphold an 1864 law that bans nearly all abortion in the state, 66% stated they strongly disapproved of the ruling. Along party lines, 82% of Democrats, 66% of Independents, and 49% of Republicans stated they strongly disapproved of the decision (Blank, 2024). Leading up to this ruling, pro-choice activists in Arizona have again pushed to get a Right to Abortion initiative on the 2024 ballot, establishing the fundamental right to abortion (Ballotpedia, 2024; Tabet, 2024). And, in the wake of the ruling, three Republicans in Arizona's House of Representatives voted with all twenty-nine Democrats on April 24, 2024, to overturn the state's 1864 law banning abortion, advancing legislation to leave the fifteen-week restriction on the procedure intact. On May 1, 2024, the Arizona Senate followed suit and voted to repeal the state's nearly one hundred sixty-year-old abortion. However, the Senate passed this bill narrowly 16 to 14, with two Republicans, Senators Shawna Bolick and T.J. Shope, voting with their Democratic colleagues (John, 2024). Following her promise to respond quickly, Democratic Arizona Governor, Katie Hobbs, signed the repeal of the 1864 abortion law on May 2, 2024, sharing that this move was "just the beginning" in the state's effort to secure reproductive health care. The events surrounding the Arizona Supreme Court upholding the state's nineteenth-century abortion ban and the legislature and executive acting within three weeks to combat the ruling are an illustration of just how polarizing and contentious abortion will remain going into the 2024 election and beyond (Snow and Lee, 2024).

It is important to keep in mind that Arizona was a contested state in the 2020 Presidential Election, where Donald Trump pressured state officials, such as Governor Doug Ducey, to overturn the results (Caldwell et al., 2023). Moreover, though Biden ultimately won Arizona in 2020, it was by a margin of under 1% (CNN, 2020). Furthermore, on April 24, 2024, an Arizona grand jury indicted Donald Trump's former Chief of Staff, Mark Meadows and attorney, Rudy Giuliani among sixteen other individuals for their involvement in trying to overturn the state's results of the 2020 election (Billeaud et al., 2024). Between the electoral controversies of 2020 that continue to be played out in state courts and the latest state Supreme Court case on abortion, Arizona is poised to be another crucial state in future elections.

The Future of Abortion Access

As discussed previously, another issue that will keep abortion a focal point in future elections is the fight over access to the procedures through non-traditional means, such as medicated abortion that can be taken at home. Again, though chemical abortion first got its approval under the Clinton Administration, access to the medication via telehealth and mail increased between 2016 and 2021, particularly when the Food and Drug Administration no longer required an in-person appointment to get a Mifeprex (mifepristone) prescription (Tumulty and Cimons, 1993; Saul, 1999; *Food and Drug Administration et al. v. Alliance for Hippocratic Medicine et al.* (2024)).

On June 13, 2024, the Supreme Court of the United States issued its official opinion on the Alliance for Hippocratic Medicine's (AHM) lawsuit against the Food and Drug Administration's (FDA) relaxation of regulations surrounding the chemical abortion drug, Mifeprex. The Court ruled in favor of the FDA, holding that the AHM and the fellow parties (i.e., the doctors and medical organization who signed onto the case) lacked Article III standing to sue the FDA (*Food and Drug Administration et al. v. Alliance for Hippocratic Medicine et al.* (2024)). The unanimous opinion, authored by Trump appointee, Associate Justice Brett Kavanaugh, covered several points by which the AHM failed to show proper standing. As discussed in Chapter 2, the concept of standing deals with a party's ability to have a court rule on the merits of their claims for which they are seeking judicial relief. To have standing, the party making the claim must show they have a true case and controversy for the court to decide. Furthermore, the party asserting the claim before the court for relief must show they have or will suffer an imminent injury, that this injury is traceable to the "unlawful actions of the opposing party," and that the injury can be redressed by a favorable judicial decision to the claimant (Constitution Annotated, 2024).

In reviewing the fifth Circuit Court's decision that held that the AHM most likely did not have standing on the FDA's 2000 approval of mifepristone and the subsequent 2019 approval on the generic version of the drug but were likely to succeed on standing for the agency's 2016 action extending the use of the medication to women who were ten weeks pregnant and the 2021 decision to no longer permit an in-person appointment for the pill, the Supreme Court ruled on several areas where the AHM failed the standing requirement. As a result, the Supreme Court reversed and remanded the lower court's ruling (*Food and Drug Administration et al. v. Alliance for Hippocratic Medicine et al.* (2024)).

First, the Supreme Court ruled that the AHM's argument that relaxing regulations on the drug would cause "downstream" conscience protection injuries to individual doctors who may be treating a patient who has taken Mifeprex and is forced to assist with their abortion is too speculative and not grounded in the facts of the record. For example, Justice Kavanaugh argued that AHM in this case is dealing with unregulated parties, in that the doctors and medical associations signed on to their claim, do not prescribe mifepristone. Moreover, Justice Kavanaugh argued that AHM did not show any evidence in the record of doctors being forced to participate in any procedures involving the drug in question and how doing so violated their conscience. Furthermore, Justice Kavanaugh highlighted how doctors in these cases are protected by the Emergency Medical Treatment and Labor Act (EMTALA) which "does not require doctors to perform abortions or provide abortion-related medical treatment over their conscience objections" (*Food and Drug Administration et al. v. Alliance for Hippocratic Medicine et al.* (2024), p. 16).

Second, the Supreme Court ruled against the AHM's argument that the doctors and medical organizations party to this case have standing because they face economic injury due to the time, they would spend diverting resources from other patients to deal with patients suffering from mifepristone complications, as well as potential increases of liability lawsuits and higher insurance costs. However, the Court ruled these claims lacked causation. Specifically, Justice Kavanaugh stated, "The causal link between the FDA's regulatory actions and those alleged injuries is too speculative or otherwise too attenuated to establish standing" (*Id.* at p. 18).

Third, the Court also ruled that the AHM did not have organizational standing because this type of standing also must meet the three requirements of individual standing before the court (injury in fact, injury caused by the defendant, and redressability). On this point, the medical associations party to the case argued that the FDA "impaired" their ability to continue their organizational missions under the relaxed mifepristone prescription scheme. The Court took issue with the medical associations' argument that because of the FDA's relaxed regulations on the chemical abortion drug, they had to expend resources in terms of reports, drafting citizens' petitions, and engaging in public advocacy on the issue. On these points, Justice Kavanaugh reminded the AHM that organizations must show more than a setback to their social interest by demonstrating concrete injuries and "cannot spend its way into standing simply by expending money to gather information and advocate against the defendant's actions" (*Id.* at p. 22).

Fourth, the Court disagreed with the AHM that they must have standing because if they don't, then no other party would be able to have standing to challenge the FDA's actions in this case. Again, here, the Court held this is too speculative of an argument by the AHM because it "is not clear no else would have standing" and that the Supreme Court has long rejected the "if not us, who?" thinking to formulate a proper standing argument (*Id.* at p. 24). Overall, Justice Kavanaugh emphasized that the AHM has a sincere moral and ideological objection to elective abortions and the FDA's policies on mifepristone; however, these objections do not establish justiciable issues before the Court.

So, what does this ruling mean for chemical and telehealth abortion going forward? Well, though the unanimous decision from the Court appears to be a victory for the Biden Administration and pro-choice advocates, it is important to keep in mind that this ruling was based on the technical issue of standing, not necessarily the merits the AHM made in their brief and oral arguments before the Court. For example, Justice Kavanaugh did not once bring up the Comstock Act of 1873 in the opinion, which was raised several times during oral arguments before the Supreme Court. As discussed in Chapter 2, this act prohibits the mailing of materials designed to induce abortion (18 USC 1461). During oral arguments when the Solicitor General, Elizabeth Prelogar, presenting the case on behalf of the government, was asked about the FDA's role in role in enforcing the Comstock Act, she argued that the act is not relevant to the FDA's authority under the Food, Drug, and Cosmetic Act. Prelogar held that nothing in the Comstock Act requires the FDA to be the agency to address restrictions about the drugs the act covers. And, that the FDA's role is limited to evaluating safety and efficacy considerations under the Federal Food, Drug, and Cosmetic Act, which gives the agency the authority to oversee the safety of food, drugs, medical devices, and cosmetics (United States Supreme Court, 2024).

Furthermore, when the case was first heard at the United States District Court for the Northern District of Texas, three states: Missouri, Idaho, and Kansas were granted status to be plaintiffs by Judge Matthew J. Kacsmaryk. However, when the case was accepted by the Supreme Court of the United States, the Court denied these states' request to intervene on the side of the AHM. However, now, these three states are looking to restart the case back at the district court, claiming they have parties facing injury in their respective states that would give them standing in court (Belluck, 2024). Since standing is a threshold issue, a party needs to demonstrate before being able to argue the merits of their case before a court; therefore, this demonstrates that these states think they have a path to still stopping access to the abortion pill through the courts.

The Supreme Court's unanimous opinion also affirms conscience protection, stating that federal law "definitively" protects doctors from being forced to take part in abortions or medical treatments that violate their conscience. The issue of conscience protection is mentioned forty-four times in the opinion (*Food and Drug Administration et al. v. Alliance for Hippocratic Medicine et al.* (2024), p. 3). This is important because it reinforces some of the pro-life arguments that call for greater enforcement of conscience protection laws in the medical and health field as another avenue to not only protect sincerely held religious beliefs but also restrict access to abortion (Whelan, 2024).

The Supreme Court's opinion is a win for now for the abortion rights activists and politicians. Yet again, the opinion does leave the possibility of this issue being raised before the Court again by a more proper party. Christian Conservative Legal Organizations (CCLOs), such as the Alliance Defending Freedom (ADF) are not giving up their legal fight to end access and avenues to abortion. As the ADF stated in the aftermath of the opinion, the Supreme Court did not address the merits of the case and the CCLO maintains the FDA's relaxed regulations on mifepristone are both illegal and harmful to women and vow to continue to "expose the reckless actions of the FDA and the harms of abortion drugs" and are "grateful" to the three states noted above for moving to take legal action to continue to hold the FDA accountable (Alliance Defending Freedom, 2024).

The abortion fight has been shifting away from the conventional in-person appointments to safe access at home for several decades. In the wake of the COVID-19 pandemic and the aftermath of the *Dobbs* decision, telehealth abortion services, which include the mailing of prescriptions such as mifepristone, have become the focus of the abortion debate, particularly with medicated abortion being used in more than 60% of pregnancy terminations across the country (Nadworny and Simmon-Duffin, 2024). With conservative states responding by prohibiting and in even some cases, criminalizing the possession of Mifeprex without a prescription, and more progressive states passing shield laws protecting physicians who provide abortions, the fight over abortion is far from over.

Federal Preemption and Emergency Abortion Access

An example of how this fight continues post-*Dobbs* can also be seen in another abortion case from the Supreme Court's 2023–2024 term, Moyle v. United States (2024). After the *Alliance for Hippocratic Freedom*, *Moyle* is the second high-profile abortion case since the overturning of *Roe* to be taken up by the Court. In the *Moyle*, the Supreme Court considered the 1986 EMTALA and if it preempted, Idaho's "Defense of Life Act," set to go into effect in August 25, 2022, making it a felony for any abortion to be administered in the state unless it was done to save the life of the pregnant mother or if they had reported themselves as a victim of rape or incest to law enforcement and could provide an official report to the physician performing the procedure (Idaho State Legislature Section 18–622, 2022). EMTALA prescribes Medicare-funded hospitals to provide essential care to patients experiencing a medical emergency *(Moyle v. United States* 2024, p. 1). EMTALA requires participants to provide stabilizing treatment if a patient experiences an acute medical condition which is so severe "that the absence of immediate medical attention could be reasonably expected to" result in serious health risks or seriously threaten bodily functions and organs (*Ibid.*). On August 2, 2022, the Biden Administration filed a lawsuit in the United States District

Court for the District of Idaho, seeking a declaratory judgment that the Defense of Life Act conflicted and was preempted by EMTALA where abortions are a necessary form of stabilizing treatment for an emergency medical condition (Department of Justice, 2022). On August 24, 2022, the District Court granted a preliminary injunction which prevented the Defense of Life Act from taking effect, holding that it was not possible for health care providers in Idaho to comply with both the state statute and federal legislation because the former obstructed Congress' intent to ensure a minimum level of emergency services. Idaho proceeded with a requesting the Ninth Circuit Court of Appeals to stay the injunction, which they denied on November 13, 2023. Idaho then asked the Supreme Court of the United States for a stay of the preliminary injunction against the Defense of Life Act. The Supreme Court granted the stay and considered the motion as also a petition for a writ of certiorari so they could hear the case (League of Women Voters, 2024).

During the period, the Supreme Court agreed to hear arguments in *Moyle v. United States* and delayed enforcement of the lower court's injunction against the Defense of Life Act, women needing to terminate their pregnancies due to medical emergencies had to be airlifted out of the state to be treated. For example, one Idaho woman whose water broke at twenty weeks, putting her at risk for infection, had to be transported out of the state to get medical attention. Idaho's Attorney General, Raul Labrador, remained skeptical of these accounts (Harris, 2024). However, multiple news outlets, such as the state's own Idaho State Journal, highlighted reports revealing that the state's largest health system was "forced to airlift patients with pregnancy complications out of the state almost every other week" (Necochea, 2024).

On June 27, 2024, the Supreme Court released its per curiam opinion in *Moyle v. United States*, holding that the writ of certiorari was dismissed as "improvidently granted," meaning, the Court should not have accepted the case. The Court also dismissed the stays on the injunction and vacated the case (Moyle v. United States, 2024, p. 1). Several justices issued concurring opinions on the case, giving insight into their posture on the Court's ruling. For example, Elena Kagan emphasized she concurred with the decision to vacate and dismiss the writ of certiorari because Idaho about EMTALA never justified emergency relief (*Id.* at p. 2). Justice Amy Coney Barrett also concurred the case should be dismissed because she believed the issued narrowed on both sides and that the petitioners raised arguments not in their original stay application. Barrett argued that the Supreme Court "should not jump ahead of the lowers courts" on this matter (*Id.* at p. 13). However, Justice Jackson while concurring with the Court's decision to vacate the stay and lift the injunction, dissented that the Supreme Court should dismiss the case as improvidently granted. Jackson argued that the conflict between Idaho and the federal government is significant and that the Supreme Court should resolve the preemption issue in this case because a clear answer on the supremacy cause escalated over the months of the case (*Id* at pp. 16–17).

Though on the surface, this opinion from the Supreme Court may look like a win for the supremacy clause, the Biden Administration and abortion rights activists, the fact of the matter is that with President Trump winning the 2024 election, this case may not get argued by the government on behalf of EMTALA. Moreover, as Justice Jackson stated in her dissent,

> Today's decision is not a victory for pregnant patients in Idaho. It is delay. While this Court dawdles and the country waits, pregnant people experiencing emergency medical conditions remain in precarious positions as their doctors are kept in the dark about what the law requires.
>
> *(Id at p. 23)*

The *Dobbs* decision made abortion access much more complex in returning the issue to the states. For the Democrats, abortion remained a focal point in the 2024 election (the first presidential election since the *Dobbs* decision). However, the reproductive freedom narrative was not enough to win the Democrats the White House. As will be discussed in the next chapter, the Republicans in 2024 were not only able to take back the presidency but also win control of Congress. The prediction now is that Republicans will take up stringent efforts over the next several years to enshrine restrictions on abortion, or even launch efforts to effect a total ban. Though some may argue that the latter may seem unlikely given its severity and the fact that 65% of Americans remain opposed to the *Dobbs* decision (Edwards-Levy, 2024). What is to be sure is that abortion will remain a top political issue for years to come, particularly because of America's complex federal system of government, where power is constitutionally divided between the states and national government. It is these factors that underscore Vice President Kamala Harris' comments when she visited the Planned Parenthood Clinic in St. Paul, Minnesota on March 14, 2024, that "one of the points that must be made on this issue, as attempt to uplift the real stories and the real consequences of the *Dobbs* decision is to remind people election matters. Elections matter" (The White House, 2024b). Chapter 5 will discuss how the dichotomy of electing Donald Trump, a "pro-life" President, can coexist with a country where the majority of Americans believe that abortion needs to be legalized in some capacity and seven out of ten states that had abortion on the 2024 ballot voted to expand access or enshrine state constitutional measures on reproductive freedom (Guarnieri and Leaphart, 2024). Indeed, American elections are complex and do matter.

References

Alliance Defending Freedom (2024) *Latest News: U.S. Food and Drug Administration v. Alliance for Hippocratic Medicine*, 13 June. Available at: https://adflegal.org/latest-news (Accessed: 15 June 2024).

Arizona Revised Statute. *§ 13–3603. Arizona State Legislature.* Available at: https://www.azag.gov/sites/default/files/docs/press-releases/2024/2024_04_18_Letter_to_health_care_leaders_re_ARS_13_3603.pdf (Accessed: 26 April 2024).

Arizona Revised Statute. *§ 36–2322. Arizona State Legislature.* Available at: https://www.azleg.gov/ars/36/02322.htm (Accessed: 26 April 2024).

Ballotpedia (2024) *Arizona Right to Abortion Initiative.* Available at: https://ballotpedia.org/Arizona_Right_to_Abortion_Initiative_(2024) (Accessed: 26 April 2024).

Belluck, P. (2024) 'The Abortion Pill Fight is Not Over. Here's What's Next', *The New York Times*, 13 June. Available at: https://www.nytimes.com/2024/06/13/us/politics/supreme-court-abortion-pill-ruling-future.html (Accessed: 15 June 2024).

Billeaud, J., Kelety, J., and Cooper, J.J. (2024) 'Arizona Indicts 18 in Election Interference Case, Including Guliani and Meadows', *Associated Press*, 24 April. Available at: https://apnews.com/article/arizona-fake-electors-charges-2020-election-9da5a7e58814ed55ceea1ca55401af85 (Accessed: 26 April 2024).

Blank, L. (2024) 'Voters Across Party Lines Disapprove of Arizona's Abortion Ban', *Data for Progress*, 16 April. Available at: https://www.dataforprogress.org/blog/2024/4/16/voters-across-party-lines-disapprove-of-arizonas-abortion-ban#:~:text=After%20being%20informed%20that%20the,%2C%20and%2049%25%20of%20Republicans (Accessed: 26 April 2024).

Caldwell, L.A., Dawsey, J., and Wingett Sanchez, Y. (2023) 'Trump Pressured Arizona Gov. Doug Ducey to Overturn 2020 Election', *The Washington Post*, 1 July. Available at: https://www.washingtonpost.com/nation/2023/07/01/trump-2020-election-arizona-governor-doug-ducey/ (Accessed: 26 April 2024).

Constitution Annotated (2024) *Article III,* Section 2, *Clause* 1.*6.1 Overview of Standing*. Available at: https://constitution.congress.gov/browse/essay/artIII-S2-C1-6-1/ALDE_00012992/ (Accessed: 13 June 2024).

Cooper, J.J. (2024) 'Democrats Pounce on Arizona Abortion Ruling and Say it Could Help Them in November's Election', *Associated Press*, 9 April. Available at: https://apnews.com/article/abortion-arizona-supreme-court-ruling-biden-democrats-361cff78974e6038e532e73e261ae8a4 (Accessed: 26 April 2024).

CNN (2020) *Presidential Results*. Available at: https://www.cnn.com/election/2020/results/president (Accessed: 10 April 2024).

Davis-Young, K. (2022) 'Poll: Most Arizona Voters Want Abortion to Remain Legal', *KJZZ.org*, 26 May. Available at: https://kjzz.org/content/1783135/poll-most-arizona-voters-want-abortion-remain-legal (Accessed: 26 April 2024).

Defense of Life Act Section 18–622. (2022) *Idaho State Legislature*. Available at: https://legislature.idaho.gov/statutesrules/idstat/title18/t18ch6/sect18-622/ (Accessed: 1 November 2024).

Department of Justice (2022) *Justice Department Sues Idaho to Protect Reproductive Rights*. Available at: https://www.justice.gov/opa/pr/justice-department-sues-idaho-protect-reproductive-rights (Accessed: 1 November 2024).

Edwards-Levy, A. (2024) 'CNN Poll: Americans Still Broadly Oppose Overturning Roe; They're Less United on What Abortion Laws Should Look Like', *CNN*, 1 May. Available at: https://www.cnn.com/2024/05/01/politics/cnn-poll-abortion-laws/index.html (Accessed: 15 June 2024).

Food and Drug Administration et al. v. Alliance for Hippocratic Medicine et al. (2024). *United States Supreme Court*. Available at: https://www.supremecourt.gov/opinions/23pdf/23-235_n7ip.pdf (Accessed: 13 June 2024).

Guarnieri, I., and Leaphart, K. (2024) 'Abortion Rights Ballot Measures Win in 7 out of 10 US States', *Guttmacher.org*, 6 November. Available at: https://www.guttmacher.org/2024/11/abortion-rights-state-ballot-measures-2024 (Accessed: 17 January 2025).

Haberman, M., Swan, J., and Lerer, L. (2024) 'Trump Privately Expresses Support for a 16-Week Abortion Ban', *New York Times*, 16 February. Available at: https://www.nytimes.com/2024/02/16/us/politics/trump-abortion-ban.html (Accessed: 10 April 2024).

Halpert, M. (2024) 'Vice-President Kamala Harris Tours Abortion Clinic in Historic First', *BBC*, 14 March. Available at: https://www.bbc.com/news/world-us-canada-68568383 (Accessed: 10 April 2024).

Harris, B (2024) 'Why Idaho's Hospitals are Having Pregnant Patients Airlifted out of State', *NBC News*, 25 April. Available at: https://www.nbcnews.com/news/us-news/idahos-abortion-emergency-supreme-court-airlifted-rcna148828 (Accessed 3 May 2024).

John, A. (2024) 'Arizona Senate Votes to Repeal Civil War-era Near-total Abortion Ban', *CNN*, 1 May. Available at: https://www.cnn.com/2024/05/01/politics/arizona-abortion-ban-senate-vote/index.html (Accessed: 3 May 2024).

Kamarck, E. (2024) 'Abortion and the 2024 Election: There Is No Easy Way Out for Republicans', *Brookings,* 17 April. Available at: https://www.brookings.edu/articles/abortion-and-the-2024-election-there-is-no-easy-way-out-for-republicans/ (Accessed: 22 April 2024).

Keenan, J.P., and Pereira, I. (2020) 'For Many White Evangelicals, the Supreme Court Makeup Solidifies Their Support for President Trump', *ABC News*, 16 October. Available at: https://abcnews.go.com/Politics/white-evangelicals-supreme-court-makeup-solidifies-support-president/story?id=73153818 (Accessed: 10 April 2024).

Korecki, N., Kapur, S., and Peter, N. (2024) ''Major hurdles': The Reality Check Behind Biden's Big Abortio Promise', *NBC News*, 19 April. Available at: https://www.nbcnews.com/politics/joe-biden/biden-big-abortion-promise-act-check-roe-v-wade-rcna146668 (Accessed: 22 April 2024).

League of Women Voters (2024) *United States v. Idaho (consolidated with Moyle v. United States)*. Available at: https://www.lwv.org/legal-center/united-states-v-idaho-consolidated-moyle-v-united-states (Accessed 1 November 2024).

Messerly, M. (2024) 'Tanden: National Ban Is GOP's 'Moderate' Position on Abortion', *Politico*, 13 March. Available: https://www.politico.com/news/2024/03/13/tanden-abortion-national-ban-gop-00146748 (Accessed: 22 April 2024).

Meyer, H., and Stanley, T. (2024) 'Conservative Christians Praise Trump's Anti-Abortion Record but Say He's Stopped Short of Goal', *Associated Press*, 8 April. Available at: https://apnews.com/article/election-2024-trump-abortion-views-conservative-evangelicals-d9a0286c809da48d65e5349cad8d1209 (Accessed: 10 April 2024).

Moyle et al. v. United States. (2024) *United States Supreme Court*. Available at: https://www.supremecourt.gov/opinions/23pdf/23-726_6jgm.pdf (Accessed: 1 November 2024).

Mulvihill, G., and Linley, S. (2023) 'Few US Adults Support Full Abortion Bans, Even in States that have Them, an AP-NOR Poll Finds', *Associated Press*, 11 July. Available at: https://apnews.com/article/abortion-poll-roe-dobbs-ban-opinion-fcfdfc5a799ac3be617d99999e92eabe (Accessed: 10 April 2024).

Nadworny, E., and Simmons-Duffin, S. (2024) 'Abortion Providers Back to 'Business as Usual' After High Court's Mifepristone Ruling', *NPR*, 13 June. Available at: https://www.npr.org/sections/shots-health-news/2024/06/13/nx-s1-5004633/abortion-supreme-court-mifepristone-ruling-pill-fda (Accessed: 15 June 2024).

Necochea, L. (2024). 'As Pregnant Idahoans Are Airlifted, GOP Doubles Down', *Idaho State Journal*, 3 May. Available at: https://www.idahostatejournal.com/townnews/legislation/opinion-as-pregnant-idahoans-are-airlifted-gop-doubles-down/article_2306a566-0971-11ef-af96-6f2f3b0b55bc.html (Accessed: 9 November 2024).

Newport, F. (2020) 'Religious Group Voting and the 2020 Election', *Gallup,* 13 November. Available at: https://news.gallup.com/opinion/polling-matters/324410/religious-group-voting-2020-election.aspx (Accessed: 10 April 2024).

Peoples, S. (2024) 'Trump's Abortion Statement Angers Conservatives and Gives the Biden Campaign a New Target', *Associated Press*, 8 April. Available at: https://apnews.com/article/abortion-trump-republican-presidential-election-2024-585faf025a1416d13d2fbc23da8d8637 (Accessed: 10 April 2024).

Planned Parenthood Arizona, Inc. et al. v. Kristin K. Mayes, Attorney General of the State of Arizona et al. (2024) *Arizona States Supreme Court, case CV-23–0005-PR*. Available at: https://www.azcourts.gov/opinions/SearchOpinionsMemoDecs.aspx?year=2024&court=999 (Accessed: 26 April 2024).

Pulliam Bailey (2016) 'White Evangelicals Voted Overwhelmingly for Donald Trump, Exit Polls Show', *The Washington Post*, 9 November. Available at: https://www.washingtonpost.com/news/acts-of-faith/wp/2016/11/09/exit-polls-show-white-evangelicals-voted-overwhelmingly-for-donald-trump/ (Accessed: 10 April 2024).

Saul, R. (1999) 'The Political Challenges and Educational Opportunities Very Early Abortion', *Guttmacher Institute*, 1 February. Available at: https://www.guttmacher.org/gpr/1999/02/political-challenges-and-educational-opportunities-very-early-abortion (Accessed: 7 May 2024).

Snow, A., and Lee, M. (2024) 'Arizona Governor's Signing of Abortion Law Repeal Follows Political Fight by Women Lawmakers', *Associated Press*, 1 May. Available at: https://apnews.com/article/abortion-arizona-women-1864-hobbs-d617843b7616c5c7f8a55424fd52dfa0 (Accessed: 3 May 2024).

Tabet, A. (2024) 'Arizona Abortion Rights Amendment Backers Says They've Gathered Signatures Needed for 2024 Ballot', *NBC News*,

2 April. Available at: https://www.nbcnews.com/politics/2024-election/arizona-abortion-rights-amendment-backers-says-gathered-signatures-nee-rcna145922 (Accessed: 26 April 2024).

The White House (2024a) *Fact Sheet: White House Task Force on Reproductive Healthcare Access Announces New Actions and Marks the 51***st** *Anniversary of Roe v. Wade*. Available at: https://bidenwhitehouse.archives.gov/briefing-room/statements-releases/2024/01/22/fact-sheet-white-house-task-force-on-reproductive-healthcare-access-announces-new-actions-and-marks-the-51st-anniversary-of-roe-v-wade/ (Accessed: 20 June 2025).

The White House (2024b) *Remarks by Vice President Harris and Doctor Sarah Traxler During Nationwide "Fight for Reproductive Freedoms Tour St.* Paul, MN. Available at: https://www.presidency.ucsb.edu/documents/remarks-the-vice-president-and-doctor-sarah-traxler-during-the-nationwide-fight-for (Accessed: 20 June 2025).

Tumulty, K., and Cimons, M. (1993) 'Clinton Revokes Abortion Curbs: Executive Orders: President Ends Ban on Fetal Tissue Research, Overturns Gag Rule at Clinics and Clears Way for the FDA to Allow Importing of French RU 486 Pill', *Los Angeles Times*, 23 January. Available at: https://www.latimes.com/archives/la-xpm-1993-01-23-mn-1587-story.html (Accessed: 7 May 2024).

United States Code Chapter 18 Section 1461. *Library of Congress*. Available at: https://tile.loc.gov/storage-services/service/ll/uscode/uscode1946-00801/uscode1946-008018071/uscode1946-008018071.pdf?loclr=bloglaw (Accessed: 15 June 2024).

United States Supreme Court (2024) *Oral Argument: FDA v. Alliance for Hippocratic Medicine*, 26 March. Available at https://www.supremecourt.gov/oral_arguments/audio/2023/23-235 (Accessed: 15 June 2024).

Ward, A. and Przybyla, H. (2024) 'Trump Allies Prepare to Infuse 'Christian Nationalism' in Second Administration, *Politico*, 20 February. Available at: https://www.politico.com/news/2024/02/20/donald-trump-allies-christian-nationalism-00142086 (Accessed: 15 June 2024).

Whelan, E. (2024) 'Some Observations on Today's Ruling in FDA Abortion-Drug Case', *National Review*, 13 June. Available at: https://www.nationalreview.com/bench-memos/some-observations-on-todays-ruling-in-fda-abortion-drug-case/ (Accessed: 15 June 2024).

Whitehead, A., Perry, S.L., and Baker, J.O. (2018) 'Make American Christian again: Christian Nationalism and Voting for Donald Trump in the 2016 Presidential Election', *Sociology of Religion*, 79(2), pp.147–171. Available at: https://doi.org/10.1093/socrel/srx070

5

DOBBS AND THE BALLOT

Two weeks ahead of the Biden–Trump 2024 Presidential Debate, *Gallup* reported that a "record-high" number of US voters, 32%, stated they would only vote for a major office candidate who held their position on abortion. This sentiment was particularly strong among Americans who considered themselves pro-choice. However, the analytics company also reported that a smaller plurality of voters, 45%, which was down eleven points from the year prior, considered abortion to be just one of many important election issues. This latter finding was the lowest reading on abortion *Gallup* had seen since 2012. Moreover, 19% of voters (up five points) shared that a candidate supporting their view on abortion was not a major issue for them (Brenan and Saad, 2024). Polls such as this and the outcome of the 2024 election suggest that though abortion was a top issue and important to many voters, it may not have been *the* motivating choice or the single issue they focused on in their voting calculation. Starting from the Biden–Trump debate through the election, this chapter will evaluate how abortion did and did not impact ballot measures and electoral outcomes in the first US Presidential Election post-*Dobbs*.

On June 27, 2024, then-President Joe Biden and Donald Trump squared off for their Presidential Debate. When asked where the candidates stood on abortion, Joe Biden affirmed his position on restoring *Roe v. Wade* (1973), which again held that women have a constitutional right to abortion. Although Trump responded that he would not support a federal abortion ban, he did take credit for appointing "three great Supreme Court justices on the court," for playing a role in overturning the landmark case, and returning the issue of abortion and its

DOI: 10.4324/9781032636177-5

regulation back to the states (CNN, 2024). Furthermore, when asked about his position on the abortion pill, which the Supreme Court ruled on just fifteen days prior to the debate, Trump recognized that the federal government still needs to be involved in this issue. Trump stated he agreed with the Supreme Court's decision upholding the Food and Drug Administration's (FDA) expedited regulation of mifepristone (again, when used with other drugs, can end pregnancy up to ten weeks of gestation) (FDA, 2024). Trump also stated that unlike some members of the Republican Party he believed in exceptions to abortion for rape, incest, and the life of mother. Biden rebutted Trump, telling him that what he had done on the abortion issue was "terrible," arguing that the majority of constitutional scholars and the public supported *Roe.* Again, this last claim is evidenced by polls showing that near the time of the debate and going into the 2024 election, six in ten Americans agreed that abortion should be legal in all or most cases (Pew Research Center, 2024a).

Pressure mounted in the weeks following the debate for Biden to step down, after both Democrats and Republicans questioned his performance, drawing attention to his lack of mental acuity, age, physical decline, and "zoned out" appearance during the exchange (Elliot, 2024). Biden's subsequent NATO press conference, his first solo one in months, also drew criticism as he referred to Vice President Kamala Harris as former President Trump and simply did not improve upon his debate performance (Williams, 2024). The press conference came on the heels of American Actor, George Clooney's opinion editorial article in *The New York Times*, where he detailed hosting a large Democratic fundraiser for Joe Biden's reelection and shared, he was concerned about the President's condition and ability to effectively continue and win the election, urging him to step aside (Clooney, 2024). Succumbing to pressure from his party, Biden announced he was dropping out of the 2024 presidential race and expressed his support of Vice President Kamala Harris, ultimately endorsing her to be the Democratic Presidential nominee ahead of the party's August convention (Han, 2024).

Many Democrats hailed Biden's decision to step aside as selfless, putting country before party (Wire and Palmer, 2024). Within days of Biden's stepping down, Kamala Harris saw a boosts in her favorability rating from 35% to 42%. And 63% of Democrats polled shared they were feeling "very enthusiastic" about her becoming the Democratic Presidential nominee (Pereira, 2024; IPSOS, 2024). On July 25, 2024, Kamala Harris, weeks before being nominated at the Democratic National Convention (DNC), launched her campaign with her first advertisement, "We Choose Freedom," featuring Beyonce's song, "Freedom," highlighting among several issues, "the freedom to make decisions about your own body," a nod to her position on securing reproductive rights (Sullivan, 2024). In the rollout of Harris' campaign, abortion became the top election issue for young women under thirty years of age (Mulvhill, 2024). However, the surge of enthusiasm among the Democratic Party and young women was not enough for Harris to defeat Trump. Is it possible that American voters wanted both less restrictive abortion rights and Trump as president?

The 2024 National Party Nominating Conventions

After the Trump–Biden debate and President Biden announcing he would not seek reelection, both major parties geared up for their respective nominating conventions. The nominating conventions take place the summer leading into the general election and play an important role in the presidential selection process. At the conventions, delegates chosen by state and local party leaders meet to choose the party's presidential nominee, which is tied to the primary and caucus election outcomes that happened in each of the states leading up to the summer conventions. (Nelson, 2011). In preparing for their convention, the Republicans revised their party's platform, particularly on the topic of abortion. Trump was able to influence a major change in the party's platform heading into the convention by getting the Committee to abandon the prior position of advocating for federal limits on abortion and instead adopting language favoring the issue to be decided by the states. Trump called into the meeting, addressing the delegates by phone to encourage them to adopt the new language and position. Some argue the state approach language is a major shift from the 2016 platform, which included advocating for a twenty-week federal limit on abortion, as well as a proposal for states to pass the "Human Life Amendment," stating that life begins at conception (Messerly et al.,

2024). As a result of Trump's advocacy and strategy for the Republicans to walk into the convention and election, leaving the issue of abortion access to the states, the platform's revised language states,

> After 51 years (arguably reference to the overturning of Roe with the help of Trump's three conservative appointees to the Supreme Court during his first term as President), because of us, that power has been given to the States and to a vote of the People. We will oppose Late Term Abortion, while supporting mothers and policies that advance Prenatal Care, access to Birth Control, and IVF (fertility treatments).
>
> *(2024 GOP Platform)*

The Democrats were also focusing on abortion ahead of their party's nominating convention in August, where the issue of reproductive rights was front and center during the four-day event in Chicago. For example, the first day of the convention, the DNC spotlighted three women and a man who shared their experiences of pregnancies and miscarriages and protections they lost due to the *Dobbs* decision. The following evening, the convention included, Kate Cox, who sued Texas in the aftermath of the overturning of *Roe* when she could not qualify for an abortion under the state law (19thNews.org, 2024). Cox's story became national news when she received a fatal fetal diagnosis from her doctor, cautioning her that continuing her pregnancy would not only pose risks to her health but also negatively impact her future fertility (Center for Reproductive Rights, 2024). Essentially, Cox did not qualify for an abortion under Texas law because it was deemed that her complications did not pose a life-threatening condition to her (Weber and Stengle, 2023). The Democrats proceeded to focus on abortion throughout the convention with including leaders from Planned Parenthood. The heavy focus on abortion politics during the convention was actually a pivot from prior years, where the strategy was to focus less on the issue during prime time coverage. Some argue that the Democrats' recent focus on abortion actually only started to emerge at the nominating convention in 2016 when Hillary Clinton was at the top of the ticket (19thNews.org, 2024).

Overall, what made the abortion issue interesting during the 2024 RNC and DNC was that the parties seemed to do a switcheroo. In prior eras, Republicans featured anti-abortion speakers, and this year they were quieter during coverage and worked with party leaders and committees behind the scenes on their party's platform language as discussed above (19thNews.org, 2024). And, Democrats, who were quieter on the issue in prior convention years (for example, Joe Biden being reluctant to discuss abortion during the 2020 convention—some say due to his Catholic faith), actually made reproductive rights arguably the theme of the 2024 DNC, thinking it would help bolster support as it did for the party in the 2022 midterm election (Bose, 2023).

For example, in addition to its featured speakers addressing abortion during the DNC, Kamala Harris' keynote speech at the last night of the event mentioned abortion four times, reproductive freedom twice, and rights for women eight times. In her remarks, the former presidential candidate warned viewers about what was a risk in terms of access to abortion, stating,

> Donald Trump hand-picked members of the United States Supreme Court to take away reproductive freedom. And now he brags about it…as part of his agenda, he and his allies would: limit access to birth control, ban medical abortion, and enact a nation-wide abortion ban…
>
> *(Harris, 2024)*

To the contrary, Donald Trump did not mention this issue of abortion or reproductive rights once during his convention speech.

Abortion and State Ballot Initiatives

So, with reproductive rights a top issue in the midterm elections and polls showing that the majority of Americans supported some form of abortion rights going into the 2024 general election, why did this issue not carry Kamala Harris to victory? Well, some argue that Americans wanted to have their cake and eat it too, meaning they wanted Trump for President and more secure access to abortion. Table 5.1 shows the states that had abortion measures on the 2024 ballot. Out of these ten states, seven passed initiatives providing legal avenues to challenge their respective state's restrictive policies, prohibiting discrimination against reproductive care and autonomy, enshrined a constitutional

TABLE 5.1 2024 State Abortion Ballot Measures

State	*Measure*	*Status*
Arizona	Proposition 139 (Right to Abortion Initiative): Enables individuals to challenge the state's fifteen-week abortion ban via establishing a fundamental right to the procedure prior to viability.	Yes: 61.61% (Passed) Result: Expands reproductive/abortion rights
Colorado	Amendment 79 (Right to Abortion and Health Insurance Coverage Initiative): Protects a constitutional right to abortion and permits the use of public funds for the procedure.	Yes: 61.97% (Passed) Result: Expands reproductive/abortion rights
Florida	Amendment 4 (Right to Abortion Initiative): Protects right to an abortion up until the point of viability or when necessary to protect the patient's health.	Yes: 57.17% (Did not pass, 60% majority required) Result: Does not expand reproductive/abortion rights
Maryland	Question 1 (Right to Reproductive Freedom Amendment): Adds article to state constitution's Declaration of Rights establishing a right to reproductive freedom and the ability to make decisions on one's own pregnancy.	Yes: 76.06% (Passed) Result: Expands reproductive/abortion rights
Missouri	Amendment 3 (Right to Reproductive Freedom Initiative): Enshrining a fundamental right to reproductive freedom, including abortion and "all matters relating to reproductive health care" to the state constitution.	Yes: 51.60% (Passed) Result: Expands reproductive/abortion rights

State	*Measure*	*Status*
Montana	CI-128 (Right to Abortion Initiative): Amended the state constitution to permit an individual the "right to make and carry out decisions about one's own pregnancy, including the right to abortion." Also permits state to regulate abortion after viability.	Yes: 57.76% (Passed) Result: Expands reproductive/abortion rights
Nebraska	(1) Initiative 434 (Prohibits Abortion After the First Trimester Amendment): Amends state constitution to prohibit abortions after the first trimester unless medical emergency, or pregnancy is a result of sexual assault or incest. (2) Initiative 439 (Right to Abortion Initiative): Amending state constitution to establish a right to abortion up until viability.	(1) Yes: 54.94% (Passed) Result: Does not expand reproductive/ abortion rights (2) Yes: 49.01% (Did not pass) Result: Does not expand reproductive/abortion rights
Nevada	Question 6 (Right to Abortion Initiative): Provides a state constitutional right to abortion, allowing the state to regulate the procedure at the point of viability, expect when to protect the life or health of the pregnant person.	Yes: 64.36% (Passed)
New York	Proposal 1 (Equal Protection of Law Amendment): People cannot be denied rights based on several characteristics, including "pregnancy, pregnancy outcomes, and reproductive healthcare and autonomy."	Yes: 62.47% (Passed) Result: Expands reproductive/abortion rights

(*Continued*)

TABLE 5.1 (Continued)

State	*Measure*	*Status*
South Dakota	Amendment G (Right to Abortion Initiative): Enshrines a state constitutional right to using a trimester framework for abortion regulation. First trimester state prohibited from regulating a woman's choice on abortion. Second trimester the state may regulate abortion in a reasonably related way to the physical health of the pregnant woman. Third trimester the state may regulate and prohibit abortion unless necessary for life and health of the pregnant woman.	Yes: 41.41% (Did not pass) Result: Does not expand reproductive/ abortions

Note: All citations for the information presented in the table are listed on the reference page

right to abortion in their state constitutions, or prohibited states from restricting access to the procedure before viability which is approximately twenty-four to twenty-six weeks of the gestational period (Guarnieri and Leaphart, 2024).

Before jumping into what the outcome of the initiatives in Table 5.1 tells us about the state of abortion politics in the 2024 elections, it is important to note that ballot measures are a form of law (The Council of State Governments, 2023). At the national level, the United States operates under the principles of representative democracy, where we elect our congressional representatives and they deliberate and vote for policy on our behalf. Twenty-four states have direct forms of democracy via the initiative process. Though the initiative process or some form of it varies by state, it allows voters to directly vote on ballot measures and affect policy (The National Conference of State Legislatures, 2023). Some argue that these forms of direct democracy may actually encourage greater political equity. For example, scholarship shows that more affluent citizens are more likely to have their preferences reflected in public policy outcomes made by elected officials than less better-off citizens . The idea behind forms of direct democracy is the hope that it promotes greater political equality by shifting the power in the policy-making process away from elites to everyday voters (Gerber and Phillips, 2003). Yet, this can be a challenging aspiration when we consider how many special interest groups insert themselves into the initiative process (Adams, 2012).

It is interesting to hold the purpose of indirect democracy and the *Dobbs* decision together in mind when processing the 2024 ballot initiatives on abortion. For example, in *Dobbs*, the Supreme Court notes thirteen times that in overturning *Roe*, they are returning the issue back to the states. Specifically, regarding the issue of abortion and democracy, the *Dobbs* opinion states, "The Court's decision today properly returns the Court to a position of neutrality and restores the people's authority to address the issue of abortion through the processes of democratic self-government established by the Constitution" (*Dobbs v. Jackson Women's Health Organization,* 2022). Out of the seven states noted above that voted to expand abortion rights during the 2024 election, four (Arizona, Missouri, Montana, and Nevada) elected Donald Trump, the Republican Candidate for President. This is interesting given that Republicans hailed the *Dobbs* decision as a major victory for abortion, hoping conservative states would react by passing laws restricting abortion. However, states noted here took the self-government ballot measure process to heart by taking the decision to protect access to abortion away from their representatives, the political elites, and placing it instead in the hands of ordinary voters to decide.

Another interesting takeaway from Table 5.1 is the state of Florida. Currently, Florida is considered a "red" state as the Republicans control both chambers of the state legislature and the governorship (News Service Florida, 2024). Donald Trump won the state of Florida by 56.1% (Associated Press, 2024). Florida's Republican governor, Ron DeSantis had over a 50% approval rating during the election season, signed the state's "heartbeat bill" in 2023, and was highly outspoken against Amendment 4, the state's abortion rights amendment, critical that it only required parental notification as opposed to consent and stating the measure would make Florida, "one of the most radical abortion jurisdictions, not just in the United States, but anywhere in the world" (Gancarski, 2024; Willis, 2024). Yet, 57.17% of Floridians participating in the election voted to pass Amendment 4. This majority fell short of the required 60% threshold required to amend the state's constitution, interestingly enough, a ballot measure that voters approved in 2006 (Varn, 2024). Despite the amendment falling short of the percentage needed to permit greater abortion access, the outcome is aligned with the majority of Americans who agree abortion should be legal in most cases (Pew Research Center, 2024b).

Furthermore, Missouri, a state that Donald Trump won by 58.5% and is controlled by Republicans, also voted to protect a fundamental right to reproductive freedom in their state's constitution with Amendment 3 (Associated Press, 2024). On December 20, 2024, the voters' choice on Amendment 3 was judicially affirmed when Judge Jerri Zhang of the Jackson County Circuit Court ruled that the state's abortion ban was "directly at odds" with the constitutional amendment that passed in November. Judge Zhang proceeded to block other state restrictions on abortion, such as the seventy-two-hour waiting period and informed consent law, requiring patients to be given various state-mandated information before receiving an abortion. However, Judge Zhang did not remove other provisions, like requiring abortion providing facilities to be licensed through the Missouri Department of Health and Senior Services (Lieb, 2024). Interestingly, another conservative states, Montana, that voted for Donald Trump to the President by 58.4%, also passed a Right to Abortion Initiative, safe guarding a woman's ability to make decisions about their pregnancy, including an abortion up to the point of viability (Associated Press, 2024). So, again, among the seven states that passed pro-abortion ballot measures in 2024, four voted for Donald Trump in the 2024 election.

Having Your Election Cake and Eating It Too

As noted above, the question is, do these results indicate that voters want both less restrictive abortion rights and Trump to lead the country at the same time? Having seven out of ten states increase access to abortion is arguably a formidable win for reproductive rights, given where the nation has been since *Dobbs*. In the aftermath of the decision overturning *Roe*, over a dozen states tightened or eliminated access to abortion, and the country saw an additional fifty abortion restrictions adopted by the states (Nash and Ephross, 2022).

Oddly, Kamala Harris, who made reproductive rights the hallmark of her campaign, was soundly defeated by Donald Trump, who openly bragged about appointing three of the Supreme Court Justices who formed the majority opinion that voted to dismantle federal protections for abortion under the *Roe* and *Casey* frameworks. As abortion scholar Mary Ziegler explained to the *Los Angeles Times*, voters may not have felt like they had to choose between Trump and their position on abortion (Pinho, 2024). Again, direct democracy appears to give voters greater say over public policy, and some argue that these mechanisms can result in being more aligned with public opinion on a particular issue/ballot initiative (Arceneaux, 2002). However, some scholars are skeptical about the quality of direct democracy, arguing that it leads voters to rely on information shortcuts that require more sophistication in deliberating over the policy decision (Binder, Boudreau, and Kousser, 2011). Yet, it may be that the former reason was more at play in the 2024 election, meaning that since we know that the majority of Americans support some form of abortion, it should not necessarily surprise us that when given the opportunity to weigh in on granting or securing more access to the procedure in their states they did and this collided with the reality that most Americans simultaneously wanted Donald Trump as their President. Now, the latter choice, Trump also has the President again, is still being analyzed, and it may be that Biden held on too long and voters saw they could affect abortion politics in their states without also having to vote for Kamala Harris. These points are not the intention of this book, but suffice it to say, it does appear that voters felt they could have their cake in certain states (greater abortion access) and eat it too (vote for Donald Trump to be the President).

Abortion Politics Going Forward

Now that Donald Trump has been elected once again to the presidency, what will his administration do on abortion policy? Interestingly, abortion was not mentioned during Trump's January 20, 2025, inauguration speech. On the second day of his administration, the Department of Health and Human Services deleted abortion materials from their website, with reports indicating search for the term and Trump's policies coming up as "unreachable" (Simmons-Duffin, 2025). Yet, by Friday, January 25th, President Trump signed an executive order to end the use of federal tax dollars to fund or promote elective abortion. The order reinforces the Hyde Amendment, which took effect in 1980, restricting abortion under major federal healthcare programs like Medicaid and federal funds related to certain community health centers that provide health care services in underserved areas throughout the country (White House, 2025; Lin and Shen, 2022). Trump's executive order specifically rescinds two orders from President Biden that Trump argues violated the Hyde Amendment. Executive Order 14076 was rescinded, which promoted the Freedom of Access to Clinic Entrances (FACE) Act, "which prohibits threats of force, obstruction and property damage intended to interfere with reproductive health care services" (U.S. Department of Justice, 2023). However, Trump's order does state that federal laws protecting access to medical care for pregnant women under the Emergency Medical Treatment and Labor Act (EMTLA) and privacy of personal health information under the Health Insurance Portability and Accountability Act (HIPPS) "remain in full effect" (White House, 2025). Trump also rescinded Executive Order 14079, which his administration argues categorized abortion as "healthcare" allowing taxpayer funding to be used for elective abortion and Medicaid to pay travel expenses for such procedures (White House, 2025)

With the reelection of Donald Trump some question if he will look to Project 2025 for guidance and positioning on abortion policy. Project 2025 is a collaborative effort among conservatives to reshape government with an agenda that attacks the progressive policies of the Democrats and the Biden Administration. Largely overseen by the conservative think tank, the Heritage Foundation, the nine hundred and twenty-two-page document provides a road map to the administration for advancing conservative change in America (Project 2025, 2024; Quinn and Rosen, 2024). On the topic of abortion, Project 2025 celebrates the overturning of *Roe*, and strongly urges the next conservative President to work with Congress to implement the "most robust protections for the unborn" and deploy "existing federal powers to protect innocent life" and vigorously comply with federal bans on abortion (Project 2025, 39, 2024). Project 2025s Mandate for

Leadership mentions abortion one hundred and ninety-nine times. The manual cautions against infusing US foreign aid dollars with abortion, conditioning the use of foreign aid by having countries agree not to promote abortion, abolishing the Gender Policy Council, which they argue promotes abortion, to reserve any policies that provide abortion services for service members, to stop the use of US tax payer money to promote abortion, and reserve the US government's approval of the chemical abortion pill, just to name a few (Project 2025, 2024).

When confronted about Project 2025 on the campaign trail, then presidential candidate Donald Trump vehemently denied being part of the group or taking its recommendations. For example, when visiting the Arizona-Mexico border, Trump defended accusations by Democrats of his involvement with the group by saying, "They've been told officially, legally, in every way, that we having nothing to do with Project 25" (Giles, 2024). Yet now that Donald Trump is officially President of the United States, some argue that his executive actions on abortion and positions of incoming cabinet members overlap with the goals of Project 2025 (Contorno and Tolan, 2025).

An illustration of enacting some of Project 2025s objectives can be seen in President Trump effectively closing the US Agency for International Development (USAID), an organization that provides relief for developing countries struggling with poverty and various humanitarian issues and disasters (USA.gov, 2025). Within President Trump's first few weeks in office, his administration cut millions of dollars of funding to USAID, which impacted the agency's programs geared toward reproductive and sexual health (United Nations, 2025). In a strong showing of how the administration looks to scale back the federal government and agencies who support family planning and reproductive rights around the world, Trump took the USAID off the lease of the building it occupied, signaling essentially the end of this organization and the efforts it promoted, including those geared toward contraception and reproductive autonomy (Knickmeyer, 2025).

Again, another example of Trump appearing to implement Project 2025s pro-life mission can be seen in his presidential cabinet selections. Donald Trump's appointment of Robert F. Kennedy Jr as the Secretary of Health and Human Services (HHS) can be consequential to the FDA authorization of mifepristone, the chemical abortion pill discussed at length in Chapters 2 and 4 of this book. The Department of HHS oversees the FDA; therefore, some argue that Kennedy may make moves to repeal the agency's authorization and relax regulations of the abortion drug we saw in the aftermath of the COVID-19 pandemic and during the Biden Administration. Moreover, Kennedy has gone back and forth on abortion position, at times favoring a federal ban and then later stating he supports abortion up until a given number of weeks (Lee, 2025).

Furthermore, Trump's pick for the Commissioner of the FDA, Dr. Marty Makary, has spoken publicly about abortion, discussing how in his clinical observations as a medical student that babies resist the procedure and how it weighs on one's conscious in seeing the procedure (Knuffke, 2024). Some argue that Makary may take steps to eliminate telehealth prescriptions for mifepristone and instead return to the drug being dispensed in person or perhaps even revoke the drug entirely. If Dr. Makary was to take the latter approach, it would have a significant impact on access to abortion since medicated abortion accounts for approximately 60% of all abortions in the United States (Lee, 2025).

Additionally, Donald Trump's pick for Attorney General, Pam Bondi, is a pro-life advocate. Bondi will yield a lot of power sitting as the highest-ranking member of the Department of Justice (DOJ) and the top law enforcement officer of the United States. Under the Biden Administration, the department's Office of Legal Counsel published a memo reaffirming that the Comstock Act, which has been at the center of the chemical abortion pill debate does not prohibit the mailing of mifepristone or misoprostol (Winny, 2024; Lee, 2025). Congress passed the anti-obscenity law in 1873, which makes it a federal offense to transport by mail or common carrier "obscene" materials, such as "every article or thing designed, adapted, or intended for producing abortion, or for any indecent or immoral use" (18 USC 461, 2025). Some abortion rights scholars and activists argue that under Bondi, the DOJ may withdraw the Biden memo without issuing a new one. This could lead to uncertainty as to whether this old and obscure statutory relic from 1873 sees a resurgence and is used by pro-life advocates in the Trump Administration as a tool to restrict access to chemical abortion across the United States, as a new federal interpretation and implement of this act may preempt state laws that do not criminalize Mifeprex (Lee, 2025). When asked during her Senate confirmation hearing if she would push for restrictive federal abortion laws, Bondi responded that she would follow the law of the United States and not her personal feelings. However, time will tell how the DOJ under Bondi's leadership will handle access to Mifeprex and any possible criminalization of abortion.

Due to the *Dobbs* decision and the drastic sea of change between the Biden and Trump Administrations, the "United" States is certain to remain unified across the states when it comes to the issue of abortion for at least the next four years. This will inevitably lead to multiple court showdowns between the Trump Administration and progressive states like California, which has vowed to be "ironclad" on abortion access. For example, California legislatures have recently introduced legislation to ensure the availability of abortion pills in the event the Trump Administration looks to interfere with distribution in the state. California legislators have also introduced bills that would financially penalize cities and counties that block the building of abortion clinics. Importantly, California has a strong proponent of abortion access in the state Attorney General, Rob Bonta, and Governor, Gavin Newsom (Mays, 2024).

The fallout of *Dobbs* and the 2024 election will also pit states against one another, as conservative states intensify their efforts to penalize doctors who provide access to abortion on some level. For example, the state of Louisiana has issued an arrest warrant for Dr. Maggie Carpenter, co-founder of the Abortion Coalition for Telemedicine (ACT), a New York-based nonprofit organization, for allegedly providing abortion pills online to a pregnant minor, which is a felony in the state. Carpenter was indicted by a Louisiana grand jury. The state of Louisiana is the first state to label misoprostol a controlled and dangerous substance. The Governor of New York, Kathy Hochul refused to comply with Louisiana Governor, Jeff Landry's request to extradite Carpenter. In a case involving the same doctor, Texas did not file felony charges against Carpenter, but she was fined $100,000 penalty for breaking the state's law against teleabortion (Stengle, 2025). Overall, the trifecta for the Trump Administration and pro-life conservatives is coming together as they use the courts, favorable legal arguments in select jurisdictions, and new cabinet members to restrict abortion access not just at the federal level, but influence it at the state level as well. Unfortunately, for pro-choice activists, they will continue an uphill battle over the next four years trying to not only undo the damage of *Dobbs* put the Trump Administration on their reproductive freedom agenda. Elections have consequences.

References

19thNews.org (2024) *Abortion is Front and Center at the DNC—and the Message is About Freedom*. Available at: https://19thnews.org/2024/08/abortion-front-and-center-democratic-national-convention/ (Accessed: 9 January 2025).

Adams, B.E. (2012) 'Citizens, Interest Groups, and Local Ballot Initiatives', *Politics & Policy*, 40(1), pp.43–68. Available at: https://doi.org/10.1111/j.1747-1346.2011.00336.x

Associated Press (2024) *2024 Presidential Election Results*. Available at: https://apnews.com/projects/election-results-2024/?office=P (Accessed: 21 January 2025).

Ballotpedia (2024a) *Arizona Proposition 139, Right to Abortion Initiative*. Available at: https://ballotpedia.org/Arizona_Proposition_139,_Right_to_Abortion_Initiative_(2024) (Accessed: 17 January 2025).

Ballotpedia (2024b) *Colorado Amendment 79, Right to Abortion and Health Insurance Coverage Initiative*. Available at: https://ballotpedia.org/Colorado_Amendment_79,_Right_to_Abortion_and_Health_Insurance_Coverage_Initiative_(2024) (Accessed: 17 January 2025).

Ballotpedia (2024c) *Florida Amendment 4. Right to Abortion Initiative*. Available at: https://ballotpedia.org/Florida_Amendment_4,_Right_to_Abortion_Initiative_(2024)

Ballotpedia (2024d) *Maryland Question 1. Right to Reproductive Freedom Amendment*. Available at https://ballotpedia.org/Maryland_Question_1,_Right_to_Reproductive_Freedom_Amendment_(2024) (Accessed: 17 January 2025).

Ballotpedia (2024e) *Missouri Amendment 3. Right to Reproductive Freedom Initiative*. Available at: https://ballotpedia.org/Missouri_Amendment_3,_Right_to_Reproductive_Freedom_Initiative_(2024) (Accessed: 17 January 2025).

Ballotpedia (2024f) *Montana CI-128, Right to Abortion Initiative*. Available at: https://ballotpedia.org/Montana_CI-128,_Right_to_Abortion_Initiative_(2024) (Accessed: 17 January 2025).

Ballotpedia (2024g) *Nebraska Initiative 434, Prohibit Abortions After the First Trimester Amendment*. Available at: https://ballotpedia.org/Nebraska_Initiative_434,_Prohibit_Abortions_After_the_First_Trimester_Amendment_(2024) (Accessed: 17 January 2025).

Ballotpedia (2024h) *Nebraska Initiative 439, Right to Abortion Initiative*. Available at: https://ballotpedia.org/Nebraska_Initiative_439,_Right_to_Abortion_Initiative_(2024) (Accessed: 17 January 2025).

Ballotpedia (2024i) *Nevada Question 6, Right to Abortion Initiative*. Available at: https://ballotpedia.org/Nevada_Question_6,_Right_to_Abortion_Initiative_(2024) (Accessed: 17 January 2025).

Ballotpedia (2024j) *New York Proposal 1, Equal Protection of Law Amendment*. Available at: https://ballotpedia.org/New_York_Proposal_1,_Equal_Protection_of_Law_Amendment_(2024) (Accessed: 14 January 2025).

Ballotpedia (2024k) *South Dakota Constitutional Amendment G, Right to Abortion Initiative*. Available at: https://ballotpedia.org/South_Dakota_Constitutional_Amendment_G,_Right_to_Abortion_Initiative_(2024) (Accessed: 14 January 202).

Binder, M., Boudreau,C., and Kousser, T. (2011) 'Shortcuts to Deliberation? How Cues Reshape the Role of Information in Direct Democracy Voting,' California Western Law Review 48(1), pp. 97-128. Available at: https://scholarlycommons.law.cwsl.edu/cgi/viewcontent.cgi?article=1007&context=cwlr#:~:text=Yet%20these%20and%20other%20authors,complicated%2C%20contested%20ideal%20of%20deliberation.

Bose, N. (2023) 'Abortion Rights Center Stage in Democrats' 2024 US Election Campaign', *Reuters*, 1 September 2023. Available at: Bose, https://www.reuters.com/world/us/democrats-push-abortion-rights-heart-2024-campaign-2023-09-01/ (Accessed: 13 January 2025).

Brenan, M., and Saad, L. (2024) 'Record Share of U.S. Electorate Is Pro-Choice and Voting on It', *Gallup*, 13 June. Available at: https://news.gallup.com/poll/645836/record-share-electorate-pro-choice-voting.aspx (Accessed: 22 November 2024).

Center for Reproductive Rights (2024) *Kate Cox Tells Her Story*. Available at: https://reproductiverights.org/nyt-daily-cox-v-texas/ (Accessed: 9 January 2025).

Clooney, G. (2024) 'I Love Joe Biden. But We Need a New Nominee', *The New York Times*, 10 July. Available at: https://www.nytimes.com/2024/07/10/opinion/joe-biden-democratic-nominee.html (Accessed: 3 February 2025).

Comstock Act (1873) *United States Code Title 18,* Section 1461. Available at: https://uscode.house.gov/view.xhtml?req=granuleid:USC-prelim-title18-section1461&num=0&edition=prelim (Accessed: 10 February 2025).

Contorno, S., and Tolan, C. (2025) 'Trump Said He Hadn't Read Project 2025—But Most of His Early Executive Actions Overlap with its Proposals', *CNN*, 31 January. Available at: https://www.cnn.com/2025/01/31/politics/trump-policy-project-2025-executive-orders-invs/index.html (Accessed: 3 February 2025).

CNN (2024) *Biden-Trump Debate Transcript*. Available at: https://www.cnn.com/2024/06/27/politics/read-biden-trump-debate-rush-transcript/index.html (Accessed: 3 January 2025).

Department of Justice (2023) *Protecting Patients and Health Care Providers*. Available at: https://www.justice.gov/crt/protecting-patients-and-health-care-providers (Accessed: 29 January 2025).

Dobbs, State Health Officer of the Mississippi Department of Health, et al. v. Jackson Women's Health Organization et al. (2022) Supreme Court of the United States, Case 19-1392. Available at: //www.supremecourt.gov/opinions/21pdf/19-1392_6j37.pdf (Accessed: 1 April 2024).

Elliot, S. (2024) 'Calls for Biden to Step Aside Are About to Get Deafening', *Time*, 27 June. Available at: https://time.com/6993335/first-presidential-debate-analysis-2024/ (Accessed 19 June 2025).

Food and Drug Administration (2024) *Questions and Answers on Mifepristone for Medical Termination of Pregnancy through Ten Weeks of Gestation*. Available at: https://www.fda.gov/drugs/postmarket-drug-safety-information-patients-and-providers/questions-and-answers-mifepristone-medical-termination-pregnancy-through-ten-weeks-gestation#:~:text=Mifepristone%20is%20a%20drug%20that,of%20the%20last%20menstrual%20period) (Accessed: 3 January 2025).

Franklin, A.W. (2012) 'Management of the Problem', in S.M. Smith (ed.) *The Maltreatment of Children*. Lancaster, PA: MTP. pp. 83–95.

Gancarski, A.G. (2024) 'Ron DeSantis in Good Shape in Poll with Bad News for Other Florida Republicans', *Florida Politics*, 13 August. Available at: https://floridapolitics.com/archives/689471-ron-desantis-in-good-shape-in-poll-with-bad-news-for-other-florida-republicans/ (Accessed: 21 January 2025).

Gerber, E.R. and Phillips, J.H. (2003) 'Development Ballot Measures, Interest Group Endorsements, and the Political Geography of Growth Preferences' *American Journal of Political Science* 47(4), pp.625–39. Available at: https://doi.org/10.2307/3186123

Giles, B. (2024) 'Trump Again Distances Himself from Project 2025,' *National Public Radio*, 22 August. Available at: https://www.npr.org/2024/08/22/g-s1-19202/trump-project-2025-border-immigration (Accessed: 3 February 2025).

Guarnieri, I., and Leaphart, K. (2024) 'Abortion Rights Ballot Measures Win in 7 out of 10 US States', *Guttmacher.org*, 6 November. Available at: https://www.guttmacher.org/2024/11/abortion-rights-state-ballot-measures-2024 (Accessed: 17 January 2025).

Han, J. (2024) 'Want to Know What Biden Said When He Dropped Out? The Full Letter is Here', *NPR*, 21 July. Available at: https://www.npr.org/2024/07/21/g-s1-12544/biden-letter-withdraw-harris-endorsement (Accessed: 5 January 2025).

Harris, K. (2024) 'Democratic National Convention Speech', *PBS.org*, 23 August. Available at: https://www.pbs.org/newshour/politics/read-kamala-harris-full-speech-at-the-democratic-national-convention-2 (Accessed: 14 January 2025).

Ipsos (2024) *Most Democrats Are Very Enthusiastic About Kamala Harris as the Democratic Nominee*. Available at: https://www.ipsos.com/en-us/most-democrats-are-very-enthusiastic-about-kamala-harris-democratic-nominee (Accessed: 5 January 2025).

Knickmeyer, E. (2025) 'Trump Administration Takes USAID off Its Building Lease', *PBS*, 10 February. Available at: https://www.pbs.org/newshour/politics/trump-administration-takes-usaid-off-its-building-lease (Accessed: 28 February 2025).

Knuffke, L. (2024) 'Trump's FDA Appointment is Pro-Life', *CatholicVote.org*, 26 November. Available at: https://catholicvote.org/trumps-fda-appointment-is-pro-life/ (Accessed: 6 February 2025).

Lee, C. (2025) 'The Powers Trump's Nominees Will Have Over Abortion', *Time*, 22 January. Available: https://time.com/7209202/donald-trump-cabinet-abortion/ (Accessed: 6 February 2025).

Lieb, D.A. (2024) 'A Judge Says Missouri's Abortion Ban Isn't Enforceable, but There is No Start Date for Abortions, *WKBN*, 20 December. Available at: https://www.wkbn.com/news/national-world/ap-a-judge-says-missouris-abortion-ban-isnt-enforceable-but-theres-no-start-date-for-abortions/ (Accessed: 6 February 2025).

Lin, E.C., and Shen, W.W. (2022) 'The Hyde Amendment: An Overview', *Congressional Research Service*, 20 July. Available at: https://crsreports.congress.gov/product/pdf/IF/IF12167 (Accessed: 29 January 2025).

Nash, E. and Ephross, P. (2022) 'State Policy Trends 2022: In a Devasting Year, US Supreme Court's Decision to Overturn Roe Leads to Bans, Confusion and Chaos, Guttmacher, 19 December. Available at: https://www.guttmacher.org/2022/12/state-policy-trends-2022-devastating-year-us-supreme-courts-decision-overturn-roe-leads (Accessed 6 February 2025).

Mays, M. (2024) 'Ahead of Second Trump Term, California Vows 'Ironclad' Abortion Access', *Los Angeles Times*, 4 December. Available at: https://www.latimes.com/california/story/2024-12-04/ahead-of-second-trump-term-california-vows-ironclad-abortion-access (Accessed: 19 February 2025).

Messerly, M., Allison, N., and Sentner, I. (2024) 'RNC Committee Approves Dropping National Limits on Abortion from Party Platform', *Politico*, 8 July. Available at: https://www.politico.com/news/2024/07/08/rnc-platform-national-abortion-limits-00166788 (Accessed: 3 January 2025).

Mulvhill, G. (2024) 'Abortion Passes Inflation as Top Election Concern for Women Under 30, Survey Finds,' *PBS*, 11 October. Available at: https://www.pbs.org/newshour/politics/abortion-passes-inflation-as-top-election-concern-for-women-under-30-survey-finds

Nelson, C.J. (2011) 'The Nominating Conventions', in G. Park (ed.) *The Democratization of Presidential Elections, 1968–2008*. Washington, DC: Brookings Institution Press. pp. 45–58.

News Service Florida (2024) *A Wholesale Repudiation: The Red Tsunami that Swept Florida*. Available at: https://www.nbcmiami.com/news/local/a-wholesale-repudiation-the-red-tsunami-that-swept-florida/3467568/ (Accessed: 21 January 2025).

Pereira, I. (2024) 'Kamala Harris Sees Boost in Favorability After Joe Biden Drops out of Race: POLL', *Eyewitness News*, 28 July. Available at: https://abc7.com/post/kamala-harris-poll-vp-sees-favorability-boost-after-joe-biden-drops-out/15111289/ (Accessed: 5 January 2025).

Pew Research Center (2024a) *Public Opinion on Abortion: 1995–2004*. Available at: https://www.pewresearch.org/religion/fact-sheet/public-opinion-on-abortion/ (Accessed: 21 January 2025).

Pew Research Center (2024b) *Broad Public Support for Legal Abortion Persists 2 Years After Dobbs*. Available at: https://www.pewresearch.org/politics/2024/05/13/broad-public-support-for-legal-abortion-persists-2-years-after-dobbs/ (Accessed: 3 January 2024).

Pinho, F. (2024) 'How Both Trump and Abortion Access Won the 2024 Election', *Los Angeles Times*, 6 November. Available at: https://www.latimes.com/politics/story/2024-11-06/voters-want-abortion-and-trump-too (Accessed: 29 January 2025).

Quinn, M., and Rosen, J. (2024) 'What is Project 2025? What to Know about the Conservative Blueprint for Second Trump Administration', *CBS News*, 8 November. Available at: https://www.cbsnews.com/news/what-is-project-2025-trump-conservative-blueprint-heritage-foundation/ (Accessed: 3 February 2025).

Simmons-Duffin, S. (2025) 'Trump's Federal Health Website Scrubs 'Abortion' Search Results', *National Public Radio*, 21 January. Available at: https://www.npr.org/sections/shots-health-news/2025/01/21/nx-s1-5269875/trump-abortion-hhs-reproductive-rights (Accessed: 3 February 2025).

Stengle, J. (2025) 'New York Doctor is Fined in Texas, Charged in Louisiana Over Abortion Pills in Tests of Shield Laws', *Associated Press*, 14 February. Available at: https://apnews.com/article/abortion-doctor-maggie-carpenter-pills-847112cde026e29333c3481310593582 (Accessed: 19 February 2025).

Sullivan, H. (2024) 'We Choose Freedom: Kamala Harris Campaign Launches First Ad', *The Guardian*, 25 July. Available at: https://www.theguardian.com/us-news/article/2024/jul/25/we-choose-freedom-kamala-harris-campaign-launches-first-ad (Accessed: 5 January 2025).

The Council of State Governments (2023) *What Is a Ballot Measure?* Available at: https://www.csg.org/2023/11/02/ballot-measures/ (Accessed: 20 January 2025).

The Nation Conference of State Legislatures (2023) *Initiative and Referendum Processes*. Available at: https://www.ncsl.org/elections-and-campaigns/initiative-and-referendum-processes (Accessed: 20 January 2025).

United Nations (2025) *US Funding Cuts Confirmed, Ending Lifesaving Support for Women and Girls*. Available at: https://news.un.org/en/story/2025/02/1160631 (Accessed: 28 February 2025)

USA. GOV (2025) *U.S. Agency for International Development (USAID)*. Available at: https://www.usa.gov/agencies/u-s-agency-for-international-development#:~:text=The%20U.S.%20Agency%20for%20International,and%20engaging%20in%20democratic%20reforms. (Accessed: 28 January 2025).

Varn, K. (2024) 'Why Florida Requires 60% Approval for Constitutional Amendments', *AXIOS Tampa Bay*, 6 November. Available at: https://www.axios.com/local/tampa-bay/2024/11/06/florida-60-percent-constitutional-amendments-weed-abortion (Accessed: 21 January 2025).

Weber, P., and Stengle, J. (2023) 'Kate Cox Sought an Abortion in Texas. A Court Said No Because She Didn't Show Her Life Was in Danger', *Associated Press*, 12 December. Available at: https://apnews.com/article/abortion-kate-cox-texas-exceptions-e85664b2ab76bcb689b1b91913d3e33e (Accessed: 9 January 2025).

White House (2025) *Fact Sheet: President Donald J. Trump Enforces Overwhelmingly Popular Demand to Stop Taxpayer Funding of Abortion*. Available at: https://www.whitehouse.gov/fact-sheets/2025/01/fact-sheet-president-donald-j-trump-enforces-overwhelmingly-popular-demand-to-stop-taxpayer-funding-of-abortion/ (Accessed: 29 January 2025).

Williams, M. (2024) 'Takeaways from Biden's Critical Solo News Conference', *CNN*, 11 July 2024. Available at: https://www.cnn.com/2024/07/11/politics/takeaways-biden-nato-news-conference/index.html (Accessed: 5 January 2025).

Willis, A. (2024) 'Radical': Gov. DeSantis Speaks Out Against Amendment 4 on Abortion', *First Coast News*, 21 October. Available at: https://www.firstcoastnews.com/article/news/politics/elections/desantis-speaks-out-against-amendment-4-on-abortion/77-8b2286f2-f565-4792-9e6e-30ea8d40699a (Accessed: 21 January 2025).

Winny, A. (2024) 'The Threat to Abortion Rights You Haven't Heard of', *John Hopkins University,* 31 May. Available at: https://publichealth.jhu.edu/2024/how-the-comstock-act-threatens-abortion-rights (Accessed: 10 February 2025).

Wire, S.D., and Palmer, K. (2024) 'Top Senators, Representatives React to Biden Dropping Out of 2024 Election', *USA Today*, 21 July. Available at: https://www.usatoday.com/story/news/politics/elections/2024/07/21/congress-reacts-to-biden-dropping-out-endorsement-of-harris/74490865007/ (Accessed: 5 January 2025).

INDEX

Note: **Bold** page numbers refer to tables.

Abington v. Schempp (1963) 3
"Abolition of Abortion in Louisiana Act of 2022" 52–53
abortion 1, 25; ban on 83; and democracy 105; future of access 85–89; multifaceted issue 70; and Party politics 2–6; political debate on 2; Republican Party on 4–5; and state ballot initiatives 101, **102–104**, 104–106
Abortion Coalition for Telemedicine (ACT) 111
abortion pill 26, 27, 32, 37, 41, 98; chemical 32–33; as controlled substances 68; Red states *versus* Blue states 68; RU-486 30, 41–45
abortion policies, religious influence on 52
abortion politics: going forward 107–112; state of 104
abortion rights 82, 105
Abortion Rights Mobilization (ARM) 43
Affordable Care Act 13, 82
AHM *see* Alliance for Hippocratic Medicine (AHM)
Alabama Supreme Court 63
Alito, Samuel 1, 14
Alliance Defending Freedom (ADF) 8, 9, 16, 17, 26, 88
Alliance for Hippocratic Medicine (AHM) 17, 26–27, 40, 41, 85, 86; arguments by 30–33; FDA opposition to motion for preliminary injunction 33–35
Alliance for Hippocratic Medicine v. U.S. Food and Drug Administration (2023) 29
American Association of Pro-Life Obstetricians and Gynecologists (AAPLOG) 26, 34
American Bar Association 7
American Catholic Church 13
American Center for Law and Justice 8
American College of Family Medicine 26
American College of Pediatricians (ACP) 26, 34
anti-abortion activist 43
anti-obscenity law (1873) 110
Arizona-Mexico border 109
Arizona Supreme Court 82–84

Balkin, Jack 6
Barrett, Amy Coney 6, 16, 81, 91
Baylor Religion Survey (2017) 80
Benten, Leona 44
Biden, Joe 7, 97, 98, 108, 110; administration 25, 29, 32, 81–82, 87, 89, 108, 110
Biden–Trump 2024 Presidential Debate 97, 99
Bill of Rights 15

birth control 29, 42
Blue states: fight between Red and 68; Red states *versus* 66; shield laws in 67
Bob Jones University v. the United States (1983) 3
Bolick, Shawna 84
Bondi, Pam 110, 111
Bonta, Rob 111
Brown v. Board (1954) 2
Bryant, Phil 16
Buchanan, Patrick 4
Bush, George H.W. 31; administration 44
Butler Act (Tennessee) 2

Cameron, Daniel 66
Carpenter, Maggie 111
Catholic Bar Association 14
Catholic Church 2; pro-life position 4; in United States 3
Catholic Medical Association 26
CCLOs *see* Christian conservative legal organizations (CCLOs)
Center for Renewing America (CRA) 80, 81
Chemerinsky, Erwin 28
chemical abortion 30–32; lobbying over 41–45
chemical abortion drug 32–34, 36, 85, 87, 109; generic version of 34; in-person dispensing requirement of 37
chemical drug abortion regimen 31, 32
Christian and Dental Association 26
Christian Conservative Legal Organizations (CCLOs) 5–10, **11–12**, 13–14, 16, 17, 26, 28, 88
Christian Legal Movement 6–10, 25–26
Christian Medical Association (CMA) 34
Christian nationalism 80, 81
Christian Right movement 2, 3, 5, 10, 16
Clinton, Bill 45; administration 30, 31, 85
Clinton, Hillary 100
Clooney, George 98
Code of Federal Regulations 31
Cohen, D.S. 70
Comstock Act (1873) 87, 110
conservative states 63, 64, 66, 67, 69
Coptic Medical Association 26
COVID-19 pandemic 27, 32, 35, 41, 89, 109, 110
Cox, Kate 64, 100
Currie, Becky 16
CVS 66, 67

Danco Laboratories 39, 40, 42
Defense of Life Act 89, 90
Democratic National Convention (DNC) 99–101
Democratic Party 4, 5, 25, 50, 83, 84, 98, 100, 101, 108, 109
Dennis, C. 51, 52, 66
Dickman, S. 70
District Court ruling, aftermath of 38–41
Dobbs decision 69, 80, 81, 89, 91, 100, 105, 111; aftermath of 66, 70; consequences of 70
Dobbs era politics 7
Dobbs v. Jackson Women's Health Organization (2022) 1, 7, 9, 14
Dobson, James 8
drugs: chemical abortion 31; REMS and in-person dispensing of 34; RU-486 30
Ducey, Doug 84

emergency abortion access 89–92
Emergency Medical Treatment and Labor Act (EMTALA) 86, 89–91, 108
Engel v. Vitale (1962) 3
Equal Rights Amendment (ERA) 4
Erie Doctrine 27–30
Evangelical Protestants 1–3, 8, 13
Executive Order 14079 108

Falwell, Jerry 2, 5, 8
Family Planning Services and Population Research Act (1970) 42

Federal Food, Drug, and Cosmetic Act 31, 33
Federalist Society 7
federal preemption 89–92
Feminist Majority Foundation (FMF) 43
fetal personhood 64
First Liberty Institute 28
Food and Drug Administration (FDA) 26, 30, 67, 85, 98; opposition to AHM's motion for preliminary injunction 33–35
Food and Drug Administration, et al., v Alliance for Hippocratic Medicine, et al. 40
Food, Drug, and Cosmetic Act 87, 88
forum shopping 27–30
Fourteenth Amendment 14, 15
Freedom of Access to Clinic Entrances (FACE) Act 108

Gainsbourg, Ruth Bader 6
Gallup 97
Gender Policy Council 109
Gestational Age Act 16
Giuliani, Rudy 84
Gordon, Mark 68
Gorsuch, Neil 6, 7, 16, 81
Graham, Lindsey 81
Grand Ole Party (GOP) platform 4
Greene, David 14
Griswold v. Connecticut (1965) 15

Harris, Kamala 82, 92, 98, 99, 101, 107
Health Insurance Portability and Accountability Act (HIPPS) 108
Heckler v. Chaney (1985) 37
Hobbs, Katie 84
Hochul, Kathy 111
Hoosiers Jews for Choice 65
Howell Code 83
"Human Life Amendment" 99–100
Hyde Amendment 108

Indiana Court of Appeals 65
Indiana Religious Freedom Restoration Act 65, 66; KRS §446.350 65
in-person dispensing 34, 35; requirement of chemical abortion pill 37
Internal Revenue Service (IRS) 2, 3, 5, 10
in vitro fertilization (IVF) 63, 64

Jackman, J. 43, 44
Jackson, Justice 91
Jewish faith 65, 66
Johnson, Mike 82
Jones, Bob 5
judge shopping 27–30
jurisdiction 27–28

Kacsmaryk, Matthew J. 27–29, 38, 88; district court order and opinion 36–38
Kagan, Elena 90
Kansas' House Bill 2749 69
Kavanaugh, Brett 1, 7, 16, 68, 69, 81, 85, 87
Kelly, Laura 69
Kennedy, Dennis James 8
Kennedy Jr., Robert F. 109, 110

Labrador, Raul 90
Lader, Lawrence 44
Lake, Kari 81
Lambert, V.C. 52
Landry, Jeff 67, 111
Leo, Leonard 7
Lewis, A. 8, 41, 66
"Lochner era" 15

Makary, Marty 110
Masterpiece Cakeshop v. Colorado Civil Rights Commission (2018) 8
McGovern, George 4
Meadows, Mark 84
Medi-Cal 67
Medoff, M. 51, 52, 66
Mifeprex (mifepristone) 30–32, 34–36, 38, 39, 67, 85, 86, 110; approval of 36, 39; "Non-Enforcement Decision" on 32; to United States 43
misoprostol 30, 67

Moral Majority 3, 5, 8
Moyle v. United States (2024) 89–90

National Abortion and Reproductive Rights Action League (NARAL) 43
National Association for the Repeal of Abortion Laws (NARAL) 5
National Association of Prolife Nurses 26
National Center for Population and Family Planning 42
National Legal Foundation 8
National Party nominating conventions (2024) 99–101
National Right to Life Committee 5, 43
National Women's Health Network 43
negative effect abortion 52
Newsom, Gavin 67–69, 111
Nguyen, D. 70
Nixon, Richard 4, 42
Non-Enforcement Decision 39

Oldmixon, E. 51, 52, 66

Party politics: abortion and 2–6
Paxton, Ken 64
Pediatric Research and Equity Act 31
plaintiffs 27, 30, 34–37, 65
Planned Parenthood (PP) 43
Planned Parenthood v. Casey (1992) 1, 50
Political Action Committees 5
population control movement 42
Population Council 42, 43
Population Crisis Committee 43
Population Movement 42
post-*Dobbs* America 50; new legal battles in 17–18; unintended pregnancies in 70
pregnancy 26, 30, 31, 38
Prelogar, Elizabeth 87
pro-Choice movement 43
Project 2025 108–109
pro-life movement 13, 64

Rabbinic tradition 65
Reagan, Ronald 3, 5, 7
Red states: *versus* Blue states 66; fight between Blue and 68
religious conservatives 2, 8
Religious Freedom Restoration Act (1993) 14
religious language/beliefs 65
Reproductive Health and Technology Project (RHTP) 43
reproductive rights 25–45, 107
Republican Party 50, 83, 84, 98, 101; on abortion issue 4–5
Right to Abortion initiative 84
Risk Evaluation and Mitigation Strategy (REMS) 34
RNC 100
Robertson, Pat 8
Rockefeller Brothers Fund (1952) 42
Rockefeller III, John D. 42
Roe v. Wade (1973) 1, 3, 8, 9, 13, 16, 42–43, 50, 80, 82, 83, 97
Roussel Uclaf 42–44
RU-486 30–31, 41–45

saliency 51, 52
Scopes, John T. 2
Scopes "Monkey" Trial (1925) 2
Senate Bill 276 67
Senate Bill 345 69
Senate Bill 385 69
Shope, T.J. 84
sixteen-week national abortion ban 81
Social Security Act 42
state ballot initiatives 101, **102–104**, 104–106
Subpart H process 31, 33, 36, 38

targeted regulation of abortion providers (TRAP) 51–52
telehealth abortion services 68, 70, 89
Texas Supreme Court 65
Thomas, Clarence 14
Thomas More Society 14

Travis County District Court 64
Trinity Lutheran Church of Columbia, Inc. v. Comer (2017) 9
Trump, Donald 7, 81, 83, 84, 97–100, 105–110; administration 110–112; electoral success 80

unintended pregnancies, in post-*Dobbs* America 70
United States: Catholic Church in 3; chemical abortion in 30, 110; Christian Right and evangelical movement in 5; conservative Christian legal organizations in 10, **11–12**; drugs in 31; mifepristone to 43; political debate on abortion in 2; principles of representative democracy 104; restrictive and protective access to abortion in 50, **53–62**
United States Conference of Catholic Bishops (USCCB) 13, 14
US Agency for International Development (USAID) 109
US Court of Appeals for Fifth Circuit 16, 36, 38, 39
US feminist groups 43
U.S. Food & Drug Administration v. Alliance for Hippocratic 40
US Supreme Court 1–3, 6, 7, 9, 14, 16, 39–41, 43, 44, 81, 83, 85, 86, 88, 89–91, 105

venue 28
Vought, Russell 80

Waggoner, Kristen 7
Walgreens 66–67
Washington Post 29
Wheeler, R. 29
Whitehead, A. 80
Wolfe, William 81
World War II 42
"Wrongful Death of a Minor Act" 63

Yamane, D. 51, 52, 66
Young, Frank 43

Zhang, Jerri 106
Ziegler, Mary 107

Kolibri 360 GmbH
Ferdinand-Jühlke-Straße 7
99095 Erfurt, Deutschland
produktsicherheit@kolibri360.de